ARCANUM BOOKS series

CW00920076

Gateways to Otherworld is the eighth title published in Ignotus Books. *Arcanum* books are titles of under 100-pages of practical and/or instructional text on a specific esoteric subject or theme and written by magical practitioners with proven antecedents. Based on the idea of those children's 'Ladybird' books that often introduced us to an interest that lasted a life time and, taking its name from the Coven of the Scales' foundation course, the aim is to offer further tuition/guidance on specific elements of witch-lore and practice.

Coming in at under 25,000 words, each title will be packed with information and instruction rather than puffed out with superfluous wordage and regurgitated text borrowed from other publications. The series will be aimed at those who have attained a certain level of magical competence and who don't need to be spoon-fed basic instructions for Circle-casting with each volume– and are therefore not written with beginners in mind.

Sacrifice to the Gods
Talking to Crows
Hagstones
Thrice Great Thoth
Treasure House of Images
Quartz: Breath of the Dragon
Scent of the Witch
Gateways to Otherworld

Dedicated to Heather and Steve
who share my sentiments ...

*'I would rather live in a world where my life is
surrounded by mystery
than live in a world so small that my mind could
comprehend it'*
Harry Emerson Fosdick

Gateways to Otherworld

Melusine Draco

Published in 2021 by ignotus press UK

A CIP catalogue record for this title is available from the British Library.

Cover image by BonnyBBX (Mystic Art Design) from Pixabay

4

CONTENTS

Chapter One: Otherworld

When we talk of Otherworld, we are usually referring to the world of spirit, of Fae, and the ancient Ancestors, where *kindred calls to kindred and blood calls to blood*. It is a separate reality, or a world that exists simultaneously with ours, but independent of it – and most true witches find that they spend their lives with one foot in the 'real' world and one foot in Otherworld.

We co-exist in a way that enables us to 'see' things on the other side of the veil without the rigmarole of trance- or path-working, self-hypnosis, meditation or contemplation. To find psychic gateways or portals that enable us to step through into an Otherworld that is as clearly defined as stepping through our own front door, and enhanced by our ability to perceive the subtle-dimension – or the unseen world of spirit.

Otherworld *is* the world of 'spirit' in its widest possible sense as Bob Clay-Egerton explained: that there are innumerable planes of existence on different levels in many dimensions. Mankind exists, physically, in one dimension of time and space. Mentally he can penetrate to other levels. Spiritually he can reach even more. "This is similar to a trained pearl or sponge diver being able to reach very much greater depths, for longer periods, than can the untrained diver – who can, nevertheless, reach greater depths in safety than a non-swimmer.

As mankind can mentally and spiritually penetrate to

other levels, so other entities can penetrate to our level, in our dimension. And, as not all men and women are benevolent, so not all intruding entities are kindly; as men and women differ in intelligence, so do the entities of other planes. Thus we have a variety ranging from simple, uncomplicated 'elemental' entities to complex and powerful 'deific' or Ancestral entities."

The terms gateway, portal and doorway speak for themselves, and as a witch's magical ability develops these psychic 'gateways' will begin to open – maybe in one, or even several directions simultaneously. Personal advancement along the Old Craft path depends on an individual's willingness to pass through or stay put, since these gateways open as a result of personal progress serving as an indication that the time has come to move on and climb to the next level.

Sometimes this transition can be difficult and painful but in magical learning, everything has a reason (and a price!), so we must never ignore the opportunity, no matter how strange or vague it may seem. The price of an Old Craft witch's progress can seem exacting but the end result is well worth the trial; to ignore it will only result in *personal* loss in terms of both spiritual and magical development. In time, the same situation may return and the trial begins all over again. If the opportunity is not taken, it could be many years along the line before it occurs again, in which case there are many years lost in an individual's advancement as it will be akin to starting anew; or it may not occur again in this lifetime.

Gateways or portals can appear in Circle; during meditation; or in a dream, but we should not be afraid of these blinding flashes of awareness, as they only appear when the 'powers that be' feel we are ready to encounter them. For an experienced witch, it may be a boot in the bustle to suggest they've spent long enough in a particular comfort zone and that it's time to take the next step.

8

Not taking advantage of these new openings will be the individual's forfeiture, since those who have chosen *not* to pass through these gateways – even after many years of practice – often remain at exactly the same spiritual level as when they first began. Their magical development and the understanding of it has never altered; their progression halted due to their own fears and misunderstanding. They have tried to batter down the door for years without success; while the true Elder Faith witch finds that the gate swings open at just the lightest touch of a finger when the time is right.

Passing through the portal also brings awareness that there are all manner of other different currents and movements on the planet that affect us on a deeper magico-mystical level [*Traditional Witchcraft and the Path to the Mysteries*]. Let us consider for a moment Professor Brian Cox's comment that every blade of grass has 3.8 billion years of history written into it. Or what we often blithely refer to as 'earth mysteries' that can produce a mild tingling sensation, which sets the pendulum swinging. Or a burst of warm energy in our hands and feet when we stand in close proximity to ancient megaliths.

The concept of an Otherworld in historical Indo-European and Old Europe religions is reconstructed in comparable mythologies. Its name is borrowed from *orbis alius* (Latin for 'other Earth/world'), a term used by Lucan in his description of the Celtic Otherworld. Comparable religious, mythological or metaphysical concepts, such as a realm of supernatural beings and a realm of the dead, are found in cultures throughout the world with an interchange of words and inter-pretations. Spirits are thought to travel between worlds, or layers of existence in such traditions, usually along an axis such as a giant tree, a standing stone, a river, a spring or a mountain path.

Many of the old Sacred Order mythologies show evidence for a belief in some form of Otherworld and in many instances, such as in Persian, Greek, Germanic, Celtic, Slavic and Indic beliefs, a river has to be crossed to allow entrance to it – and there is often a ferryman who would accompany these souls across these waters. In Greek and Indic mythology, the waters of this river were thought to wash away sins or memories; whereas Celtic and Germanic myths feature wisdom-imparting waters, suggesting that while the memories of the deceased are washed away, a drinker of the waters would gain inspiration.

The wayfarer will commonly encounter a dog in the capacity of a guardian of the Otherworld, or as the quester's guide. Examples of this are the Greek Cerberus, the three-headed hound of Hades, and the Indic Sarvarā, one of the hounds of Yama, whose names may derive from an Indo-European *kerberos* meaning 'spotted'.

In Welsh mythology and folklore, *Cŵn Annwn* (Welsh pronunciation: [*kuːn 'anʊn*], 'hounds of Annwn') were the red-eared, white-coated spectral hounds of Annwn. They were associated with a form of the Wild Hunt, presided over by either Arawn, king of Annwn in the First Branch of the *Mabinogi* and alluded to in the Fourth; or by Gwyn ap Nudd as the underworld king of the Faere Folk named in later medieval lore.

Ghostly 'black dogs' are a motif of a spectral Otherworld found primarily in the folklore of the British Isles. The black dog is essentially a nocturnal apparition, in some cases, a shape-shifter, often described as a ghost or supernatural hellhound. In English folklore, Black Shuck or simply Shuck is the name given to an East Anglian ghostly black dog which is said to roam the coastline and countryside of East Anglia, one of the many recorded in folklore across the British Isles. Accounts of Black Shuck form part of the folklore of Norfolk, Suffolk, the Cambridgeshire fens and Essex, and descriptions of the creature's appearance and nature vary considerably; it is sometimes recorded as an omen of death, but, in other instances, is described as companionable and protective.

Otherworld is depicted in many ways, including peaceful meadows, islands and buildings, making it impossible to determine how the original proto-Indo-European Otherworldly realms were viewed. The Irish Otherworld is more usually described as a paradisal fairie-land than a scary place. Many Celtic *immrams* or 'voyage stories' and other medieval texts provide evidence of a Celtic belief in a distinct Otherworld. One example which helps the reader understand the Celtic concept is the *Voyage of Bran*, first written down in the late 7th century. Otherworld is also portrayed as an island to the west in the Ocean in Celtic oral tradition, and even shown on some maps of Ireland during the medieval era.

Otherworld in the idea of Celtic beliefs became hard to distinguish and sometimes overlapped with the Christian idea of hell or heaven as this was often an analogy made to the Celtic idea, or Scandinavian idea, of a world tree. This is likely because of Roman and Scandinavian influences on Celtic cultures; red and white are the colours of animals in the Celtic Otherworld, and these colours still animate transcendent religious and mystical symbols today.

Tír na nÓg is depicted as an island paradise and super-natural realm of everlasting youth, beauty, health, abundance and joy. Its inhabitants are described as the *Tuatha Dé Danann* or the warriors of the Tuatha Dé, the gods of pre-Christian Ireland, who engage in poetry, music, entertainment, and the feast of Goibniu, which grants immortality to the participants.

In the *echtrae* (adventure) and *immram* (voyage) tales, various Irish mythical heroes visit *Tír na nÓg* after a voyage or after an invitation from one of its residents. They reach it by entering ancient burial mounds or caves, by journeying through a mist, by going under water, or by

11

travelling across the sea for three days on an enchanted boat.

The *aos sí* is the Irish term for a supernatural race in Irish mythology, comparable to the faere or elves who are said to live underground in hollow mounds, across the western sea, or in an invisible world that coexists with the world of humans. In Irish and Scottish folklore, the *aos si* (also called: *aes sidhe* – an older form of the word – and *daoine sídhe*) are a category of supernatural beings and spirits that are said to walk among the living. Much like the more commonly known faerie, they come in a variety of types with varying behaviours.

Aos si literally translates to, 'People of the Mounds', which acts as testament to their dwelling beneath the earth, or in faerie mounds (*sidhe* also translates as 'mounds'). Some believe that they come from an invisible world that coexists with our own, but remains separated by a 'veil', which means they are literally Otherworldly beings – the Ancestors, spirits of the natural world, or the Old Gods.

Needless to say, the Celtic Twilight does have its dark and shadows. When we read of the Faere Folk they tend to have an almost playful nature but it would be wrong to assume that this means those from the faerie realm are always benign. Many accounts within Irish folklore, in particular, describe people who have had a much more disturbing faerie encounter, and those who speak of these experiences are very often traumatised by what has happened to them.

Other researchers have commented upon these impenetrable happenings in the past. Indeed, the description of the inside of fairie mounds being artificially lit, as mentioned in the book *The Secret Commonwealth* by 17th-century folklorist Robert Kirk, should give us pause for thought when considering similar shamanic encounters with spirit beings from Otherworld!

There are many tales of physical retribution occurring to someone who damages a faerie tree or fort. Extreme bad luck to the extent of death is another outcome that is well known in Ireland when a person cuts down a faerie tree. Often people will suffer the consequences and only later reveal their mistake in having damaged faerie property. This is not only because people are afraid of what others will think of their beliefs, but also because the person has now witnessed the first-hand consequences of disrespecting a faerie place ... and knows that to try to avoid punishment may bring even greater wrath down upon themselves.

So, not all meetings with the Fae are light and humorous. Very often they are traumatic and full of otherworldly strangenesses which cannot be easily explained or categorised. It is no coincidence that within the Elder Faith the Fae should *not* be approached or called upon without courting the consequences.

The Brythonic forms one of the two branches of the Insular Celtic language family; the other is Gaelic. The name Brythonic was derived by Welsh Celticist John Rhys from the Welsh word *Brython*, meaning ancient Britons as opposed to an Anglo-Saxon or Gael. This Welsh tongue is the oldest language in Britain and has been spoken in some form for the last 4000 years and *Annwn* is the Otherworld in Welsh mythology.

Ruled by Arawn, it was essentially a world of delights and eternal youth where disease was absent and food was ever-abundant; located either on an island or underneath the earth. In the First Branch of the *Mabinogi*, it is implied that *Annwn* is a land within Dyfed, while the context of the Arthurian poem *Preiddeu Annwfn* suggests an island location.

Two other Otherworldly feasts that occur in the Second Branch of the *Mabinogi* are located in Harlech in north-west Wales and on Ynys Gwales in south-west Pembrokeshire. *Annwn* plays a reasonably prominent role in all four Branches of the *Mabinogi*, a set of four interlinked mythological tales dating from the early medieval period

Over time, the role of king of *Annwn* was transferred to Gwyn ap Nudd, a hunter and psychopomp, who may have been the Welsh personification of winter, because tradition revolves around Gwyn leading his spectral hunts, on his search for mortal souls. The *Cŵn Annwn* is associated with death, as it has red ears and the Celts associated the colour red with death. White is associated with the supernatural, and white animals are commonly owned by gods or other inhabitants of the Otherworld; therefore, the *Cŵn Annwn* is associated with death and the supernatural.

Tylwyth Teg (Middle Welsh for 'Fair Family'; is the most usual term in Wales for the mythological creatures corresponding to the faerie folk of English and Continental folklore, and the Irish *aos sí*. According to the folklorist Wirt Sikes, the *Tylwyth Teg* may be divided into five general types: the *Ellyllon* (elves), the *Coblynau* (faeries of the mines), the *Bwbachod* (household faeries similar to brownies), the *Gwragedd Annwn* (female faeries of the lakes and streams) and the *Gwyllion* (mountain faeries more akin to hags). The *Ellyllon* (singular *ellyll*) inhabit groves and valleys being similar to English elves. Their food consists of toadstools and faerie butter (a type of fungus); they wear digitalis bell flowers as gloves and they live in the Hollow Hills.

Surprisingly, there are six known places signposted as entry to the 'Gates to Annwn' in Wales: Ffynnone, Glaslyn, Llyn y Fan Fach, Grassholm, Pentre Ifan and the Berwyn Mountains …

- **Ffynone** is a beautiful, secluded waterfall on the river Dulas in the Cwm Cych valley. It is reputed to be the entrance to *Annwn* mentioned in the first branch of the *Mabinogion*, where Pwyll, Prince of Dyfed, discovered this beautiful place.

- **Glaslyn** (meaning Blue Lake) is in the Snowdonia National Park in Gwynedd. According to Welsh folklore, Arthur had Bedivere throw his sword Excalibur into Glaslyn, where Arthur's body was later placed in a boat to be carried away to *Afallon*. Like several other sites in Wales, it is said that if two people spend the night there, one will become a great poet while the other will become insane. A large stone known as *Maen Du'r Arddu*, below Clogwyn Du'r Arddu, is supposed to have magical powers. Llyn Coch in Cwm Clogwyn has also been associated with the *Tylwyth Teg*.

- **Llyn y Fan Fach,** meaning 'lake of the small hill,' is north of the Black Mountain in Carmarthenshire within the Brecon Beacons National Park. A folklore legend is linked with the lake, known as the Lady of the Lake. A young shepherd met a beautiful Faere woman from *Annwn*, who had ascended from the dark waters of the Lake. He took her back to his home in the nearby village of Myddfai where they married, but she warned him that if he ever struck her three times, she would go back to her underwater kingdom. She bore him three sons, but over the years he thoughtlessly struck her three times, and so she returned forever to *Annwn*; when her sons were grown, she taught them the healing powers of herbs, and they became the renowned doctors known throughout medieval Wales as the

Physicians of Myddfai. Descendants of this renowned family were still practicing medicine in the 18th century, and there is at least one herbalist in Dyfed today who claims lineage from this famous family.

- **Grassholm** (Welsh: *Gwales* or *Ynys Gwales*) is a small uninhabited island situated off the southwestern Pembrokeshire coast in Wales. Well into the 19th century it was said to be populated by a host of Faere Folk and to have a sporadic habit of disappearing beneath the sea. Grassholm has been identified with Gwales, a fabulous castle on an island featured in the *Mabinogion*. Here the severed head of Brân the Blessed (King of Britain in Welsh mythology) was kept miraculously alive for eighty years while his companions feasted in blissful forgetfulness until the opening of a forbidden door that faces Cornwall recalled them to their sorrow and the need to bury the head at the White Mount.

- **Pentre Ifan** contains and gives its name to the most significant and best-preserved Neolithic dolmen in Wales. A collection of seven principal stones, made of Preseli Bluestone from the Preseli Hills, are surrounded with a sense of something mythical, ancient and untouchable about this hill top. Also known as the 'Womb of Ceridwen' it is supposed to be one of the gateways to the land of the Fae. Stonehenge was constructed from the same stone and it is where my final resting place will be ...

- **The Berwyn range** (Welsh: *Y Berwyn* or *Mynydd y Berwyn*) is a remote and sparsely populated area

16

of moorland in the northeast of Wales, said to be the physical and geographical location of *Annwn*. There are stories of Gwyn ap Nudd and his people who live in a beautiful palace full of light, laughter, food, warmth, and how travellers on the moors of the Berwyns will sometimes suddenly be presented with this beautiful apparition and invited to join in the feasting and dancing. Anyone who chooses to do so remains in the halls of Gwyn ap Nudd, and the only way to escape is to resist temptation, declining to eat or drink

Needless to say, the same rules apply for those who are overly curious about our Otherworldly cousins – even those of us with Welsh, or a 'taint of Faere blood'. They belong to another realm and one that is very often not the safest place for humans to linger ...

As was the case in the Celtic mythologies, in Germanic legends, apples were particularly associated with the Otherworld. In the Scandinavian tradition, these mythological localities are featured in their story-telling; unlike Irish and Welsh traditions, however, an attempt was made to map the actual access points of Otherworld rather than list locales *associated* with it. In the *Edda,* many locations are named including the dwellings of the gods such as Odin's hall of *Valhalla*; or Ullr's dwelling of *Ydalar (Yewdale)*. The *Gylfaginning* and the later Norwegian poem the *Draumkvaede* feature travels into the Otherworld.

The Early Slavs believed in a mythical Otherworld where birds flew for the winter and souls went after death; this realm was often identified with paradise and it is called *Vyraj*. It was also said that spring arrived on Earth from *Vyraj*. The gates of Vyraj stopped mortals from entering and they were guarded by Veles, who sometimes took the animal form of a *raróg*, grasping in its claws the keys to the Otherworlds. *Vyraj* was sometimes also connected to the deity known as Rod – it was apparently located far beyond the sea, at the end of the Milky Way, and was usually imagined as a garden, located in the crown of the cosmic tree – where the branches were said to be nested by the birds, who were identified as human souls.

When the Slavic populations were gradually turning to Christianity, a new version of this belief became widespread in which there were two of these realms – one analogous to the original myth, a heavenly place to where birds departed, and the other an Underworld for snakes and *zmeys,* often associated with the Christian idea of hell. This second variant bears many similarities to Nav, another representation of the Slavonic Underworld.

In Classic mythology, the Greek *Under*world was where souls went after death. The original Greek idea of afterlife was that, at the moment of death, the soul was separated from the corpse, taking on the shape of the former person, and was transported to the entrance of the Underworld. Good people and bad people would then separate.

The Underworld itself – sometimes known as Hades, after its patron god – was described as being either at the outer bounds of the ocean or beneath the depths, or ends of the earth. It was considered the dark counterpart to the brightness of Mount Olympus, with the kingdom of the dead corresponding to the kingdom of the gods. Hades is a realm invisible to the living, made solely for the dead and the ancient Greeks appear to have no concept of any spirit or astral realm of Otherworld.

There are six main rivers that are visible both in the living world and Underworld; their names were meant to reflect the emotions associated with death.

- The **Styx** is generally considered to be one of the most prominent and central rivers of the Underworld and is also the most widely known out of all the rivers. Known as the river of hatred and named after the goddess Styx it river circles the Underworld seven times.
- The **Acheron** is the river of pain. It's the one that Charon, also known as the Ferryman, rows the dead over according to many mythological accounts, though sometimes it is the river Styx or both.
- The **Lethe** is the river of forgetfulness. It is associated with the goddess Lethe, the goddess of forgetfulness and oblivion. In later accounts, a poplar branch dripping with water of the Lethe became the symbol of Hypnos, the god of sleep.
- The **Phlegethon** is the river of fire. According to Plato, this river leads to the depths of Tartarus.
- The **Cocytus** is the river of wailing.
- **Oceanus** is the river that encircles the world, and it marks the east edge of the Underworld, as Erebos is west of the mortal world – a place of darkness between earth and Hades.

Entrance to Underworld:
In front of the entrance to the underworld live Grief (*Penthos*), Anxiety (*Curae*), Diseases (*Nosoi*), Old Age (*Geras*), Fear (*Phobos*), Hunger (*Limos*), Need (*Aporia*), Death (*Thanatos*), Agony (*Algea*), and Sleep (*Hypnos*), together with Guilty Joys (*Gaudia*). On the opposite threshold is War (*Polemos*), the Erinyes, and Discord (*Eris*). In the midst of all this misery, an Elm can be seen where false Dreams (*Oneiroi*) cling under every leaf. Close to the doors are many beasts, including Centaurs, Scylla, Briareus, Gorgons, Geryon, the Lernaean Hydra, the Chimera, and Harpies.

The souls that enter the underworld carry a coin under their tongue to pay Charon to take them across the river, although he may make exceptions or allowances for those visitors carrying a Golden Bough (mistletoe). Although Charon ferries across most souls, he does turn a few away. These are the unburied which can't be taken across from bank to bank until they receive a proper interment. Across the river, guarding the gates of the underworld is the three-headed dog, Cerberus, beyond whom is where the Judges of the Underworld decide where to send the souls of the dead – to the Isles of the Blessed (Elysium), or Tartarus.

While **Tartarus** is not considered to be directly a part of the underworld, it is described as being as far beneath the underworld as the earth is beneath the sky. It is so dark that the 'night is poured around it in three rows like a collar round the neck, while above it grows the roots of the earth and of the unharvested sea'. Zeus cast the Titans along with his father Cronus into Tartarus after defeating them and Homer wrote that Cronus then became the king of Tartarus. While Odysseus does not see the Titans himself, he mentions some of the people within the underworld who are experiencing punishment for their sins.

The **Asphodel Meadows** were a place for ordinary or indifferent souls who did not commit any significant crimes, but who also did not achieve any greatness or recognition that would warrant them being admitted to the Elysian Fields. It was where mortals who did not belong anywhere else in the underworld were sent.

In the *Aeneid*, the **Mourning Fields** (*Lugentes Campi*) was a section of the underworld reserved for souls who wasted their lives on unrequited love. Those mentioned as residents of this place are Dido, Phaedra, Procris, Eriphyle, Pasiphaë, Evadne, Laodamia, and Caeneus.

Elysium was a place for the especially distinguished. It was ruled over by Rhadamanthus, and the souls that dwelled there had an easy afterlife with no labours. Usually, those who had proximity to the gods were granted admission, rather than those who were especially righteous or had ethical merit, however, later on, those who were pure and righteous were considered to reside in Elysium. Most accepted to Elysium were demigods or heroes; heroes such as Cadmus, Peleus, and Achilles were transported here after their deaths. Normal people who lived righteous and virtuous lives could also gain entrance such as Socrates who proved his worth sufficiently through philosophy.

The **Fortunate Isles** or *Isles of the Blessed* were in the realm of Elysium. When a soul achieved Elysium, they had a choice to either stay in Elysium or to be reborn. If a soul was reborn three times and achieved Elysium all three times, then they were sent to the Isles of the Blessed to live in eternal paradise. As the Elysian Fields expanded to include ordinary people who lived pure lives, the Fortunate Isles then began to be considered the final destination for demigods and heroes.

Generally speaking, Otherworld can be defined as a plane of existence populated by spirit entities, the Ancestors, guardians, numen, *genii loci*, nature sprites, the Faerie, discarnate entities, *et al*. What we must never lose sight of is the fact that these energies/entities can be helpful or harmful, and should be treated with the greatest respect and caution.

These are cosmic energies on a very low level but they are far more powerful than can ever be imagined and, as such, can destroy if treated in a cavalier manner. These elemental beings actually exist, and imbued with an intellectual reasoning akin to the Earth, Nature and the Landscape that is very, *very* real.

Magically and mystically, it is essential we learn to understand as much about these separate and distinct

21

energies/intelligences as possible and why in Coven of the Scales using eclectic mix-and-match god-forms from different cultures is *not* encouraged. Once summoned, any entity requires energy on which to feed (i.e. 'charge its own batteries') and if not kept under firm control, or the magical working not closed down correctly, it may continue to feed and grow until it manifests into something unpleasant and difficult to shift – which is not as rare as we would like to admit!

Whatever we call these 'powers' they *do* have the necessary link to the abilities and attributes that we strive for in the hopes of finding all we seek. If the invocation is gone about in the right manner, there is no reason why this cannot be achieved – but it must be constantly borne in mind that these entitites are not interested in any human development, only their own.

Only by encountering these varying agencies can we learn to differentiate between the positive/negative, active/passive beings that exist on other planes because for every one that will help, guide and give advice, there is the same number who will hinder, deceive and cause harm, if given the opportunity.

There are times, however, when the way is barred to us for no apparent reason. As Crowley is his wisdom observed: 'Physical ability and moral determination count for nothing. It is impossible to perform the simplest act when the Gods say 'No'. I have no idea how they bring pressure to bear on such occasions; I only know that it is irresistible. One may be wholeheartedly eager to do something which is as easy as falling off a log; and yet it is impossible.'

We will encounter this sensation time and time again on a mystical quest on both the physical and astral planes, when an invisible barrier prevents us from going further. The reason is that no sooner does an individual make up their mind to step onto the Path of the Elder Faith than they automatically arouse the supreme hostility of every force, internal or external, in their sphere. We push against the barrier and rail against the unfairness but the way remains shut; perhaps our Guardian has thrown up a protective shield for some reason best know to itself – but in time the barrier dissolves – again for no apparent reason – and at the slightest touch the door swings open – and we are free to go on our way.

The source for the material contained in the Coven of the Scales teaching is based on that from a British-based Old Craft coven led by Aleister (Bob) and Mériém Clay-Egerton that could trace its roots in Cheshire, England, back to the 1800s. Their view was that it is not unreasonable to surmise that the Elder Faith probably retains features of the native shamanic practices of the ancient Britons, since the term 'shamanism' describes the supernatural powers practitioners channel from the spirit world for healing, divination and the conducting of souls

All of which are the natural province of an Old Craft practitioner where it is viewed as '*an isolated or peripheral phenomenon*', rather than the overt devotional practices often found in contemporary paganism. As intermediaries between the world of the Ancestors and the living, the Old Craft practitioner maintains *direct* contact with spirits, whether of Otherworld, 'of plants, animals and other features of the environment, such as the "master-spirits" (e.g. of rivers or mountains)'.

Much of this may be seen as playing with semantics, but in truth, the god-forms themselves have changed greatly down through the millennia. It is only by studying myths, legends and folklore, and pulling all the strands together that we can appreciate just how much these *have* altered.

The spirits of the landscape, however, have remained constant; they have not altered their form and have only grown more powerful with age. These well-springs of magical energy have not been contaminated because few have known of their existence – apart from the native shamanic practitioners of the Elder Faith who have kept the secret down through the ages.

In more secluded spots, the spirit-energy of the ancient Britons survives in remote ancient monuments, isolated lakes, the rural landscape, and in the depths of the surviving wildwood, with which our hunter-gatherer Ancestors would have been familiar. When the native shamanic practices went into the shadows, these powerful energy spots were deemed unholy and feared by the locals – and as such passed into folklore as those things that are 'never fully remembered and yet never fully forgotten'.

For our first step in seeking out these 'energy spots' we need to start looking at the local landscape through different eyes if we want to find the secret portals to Otherworld. Those other realms of existence beyond the world of mankind, especially the spirit realms of the nature sprite or the Faere Folk that are cunningly concealed in the field margin, at the bend of a stream, in the light on the hillside or in the shadows of the trees. Portals that are more evident at certain times of the day (twilight), or month (full moon), or year (the solstices and equinoxes) when the veil between the worlds is at its thinnest. Or as Evan John Jones wrote …

One concept was learned, but behind that was another hidden mystery. The lifting of one veil led to the finding of yet another. At the same time, one was left knowing that behind all these veils was an inner core, a hidden truth that only the very few would ever find. I have yet to reach that stage – if I ever do. But the sureness of its being there, and the knowledge that it is, can be reward enough in itself.

[*Witchcraft: A Tradition Renewed*]

Chapter Two: A Liminal Space Moment

Otherworld exists parallel to the world of the living separated only by that flimsy veil, so boundaries often become blurred and easier to cross. The concept of an 'Otherworld' in what can best be described as 'proto-Indo-European beliefs' can be found in the comparative faiths of those cultures.

Comparable mythological, religious or meta-physical concepts, such as a realm of supernatural beings thought to travel between worlds, or layers of metaphysical existence are also found in various different ethnicities across the globe. And we usually find that those with a life-long attachment to this esoteric spirit-land have lived with one foot in Otherworld since they were children, because this is also the realm of the Ancestors.

Needless to say, the interpretation of Otherworld is not clearly defined because the denizens of those realms are nebulous, unpredictable, capricious and often downright dangerous. This is the domain of the fae, *numen*, elementals, nature sprites and other supernatural forces beyond scientific understanding or even sometimes seen as the laws of Nature.

Contrary to what we would like to believe, many of these entities are openly hostile to humans whom they hold responsible for the destruction of the Earth and their own displacement within its woods, mountains, lakes and forests. Therefore it would be unwise to take their acceptance for granted simply because *we* view ourselves as fully-fledged, card-carrying members of the pagan community, and be aware of any barrier or sentinel blocking the way – abiding by their rejection with good grace – until the next time.

Whenever we go out into the countryside, or even some less-densely populated urban areas, we may notice there *are* certain places or 'states of being' with which we feel different, uncertain, or uncomfortable. Often, these uncomfortable spots may turn out to be liminal spaces; the word coming from the Latin *limen*, meaning 'threshold' – that is, any point or place of entering or beginning. A liminal space is the time between times – the 'what was' and the 'next'.

It is a place of transition, of waiting, and not knowing; often physical locations such as a field margin, a double-hedge, a river bank, or a clearing in the woods can produce these sensations. In some cases, the same place may be at one time liminal and, at other times not. Other places may have the feeling of being liminal around a certain time of day, or season, when we visit them – especially around the Solstices and Equinoxes.

Often, whenever we visit a place during a time when it's not usual for us to be in that particular spot, it can feel unsettling – as if we've gate-crashed a party. Or, if we're in a place for longer than necessary when we're passing through to our actual destination, we may experience that same feeling of something being out of kilter that we can't quite pinpoint – as if we've out-stayed our welcome, or arrived unexpectedly.

The liminal veil is what we call the place where a transition occurs between the threshold and the place that waits *beyond*. It may briefly feel confining, but often it takes only minor adjustments to get through to the next plane and this is where we often encounter entities from Otherworld.

In magical practice, particularly during Initiation, liminality is the quality of ambiguity or disorientation that occurs in the middle stages of the rite, when participants no longer hold their pre-ritual status but have not yet begun the transition to the status they will hold when the rite is complete. During a rite's liminal stage, participants stand at the threshold between their previous way of structuring their identity, time, or community, and a new way, which the rite establishes.

Hence the warning about the dangers when subjecting ourselves to undergoing such ordeals, that we either come out the other end mad, dead or enlightened. If we don't experience these sensations of personal change or transition, then we should accept that it probably 'didn't take' and that we need to go back to the beginning and start again! Development in the Elder Faith is all about new beginnings and starting over …

What we call the beginning is often the end
And to make an end is to make a beginning.
The end is where we start from.

We often get asked why a large number of Craft celebrations are held on the night *before* an event – such as Mid-Summer Eve rather than the night of Mid-Summer Day. In the ancient world, the day was observed from sunrise to sunrise and the night belonged to the day that came *after* – just as we refer to Mid-Summer Eve, Mid-Summer Day and Mid-Summer Night, the setting for Shakespeare's *Mid-Summer Night's Dream* – with all their different observances.

The Romans were, for example, originally an agrarian people and just as their year revolved around the seasons, their daily life was organised relative to the position of the sun in the sky. The day began at sunrise (*solis ortus*); this was preceded (i.e. before the day started) by about thirty minutes of twilight (*diluculum*) that followed first light (*prima lux*).

All this is, of course, related to natural history – simply because all animals and plant life becomes active with

27

sunrise, the original start of day, while at dusk things will start closing down. In between was the midday, signifying maximum Sun or the life-affirming force moving the seas, planet, life, etc – on the other hand, midnight was the deepest time when the life-affirming force was missing.

Nocturnal creatures were therefore seen as going against natural laws. The 'witching hour' – accompanied by shadows, tricks of the light and strange shapes that suddenly, somehow appear more eerie than usual, were said to come into their own at this time. Once again, it is the understanding of these things that strengthens our link to the Ancestors, when we can explore this liminal space – this time between times – that occurs at various intervals during the day.

When, for example: *kindred calls to kindred, blood calls to blood.*

Dawn: From an Old English verb *dagian*: 'to become day' and marking the beginning of the morning twilight before sunrise. Dawn begins with the first sight of light in the morning, and continues until the sun breaks the horizon, with many Indo-European mythologies having a dawn goddess, separate from the male solar deity … including a phenomenon known as the 'false dawn'.

Twilight: In the morning, twilight begins when the sun is just below the horizon and ends at sunrise. We can define twilight simply as the time of day between daylight and darkness, whether that's after sunset, or before sunrise, when the light from the sky appears diffused and often pinkish. The sun is below the horizon, but its rays are scattered by Earth's atmosphere to create the colours of twilight. The 'blue hour' refers to the darker stages of both morning and evening twilight, when the Sun is far below the horizon, colouring the sky deep blue.

Sunrise: The term commonly refers to periods of time both before and after this point, although astronomically, sunrise occurs for only an instant: the moment at which the upper edge of the sun appears touching but intersecting the horizon. The ancient day was calculated from sunrise to sunset.

Noon: Synonymous with midday, which is a slightly different concept and points to the middle of the daylight period. Noon and midday may not be at the same time, as in astronomical terms, it is the moment when the sun crosses the local meridian and reaches its highest position in the sky except at the poles – also called high noon.

Sunset: Also known as sundown, the time of sunset varies throughout the year and is the daily disappearance of the sun below the horizon due to Earth's rotation. The time of sunset is defined in astronomy as the moment when the upper edge of the Sun disappears below the horizon and the traditional time for coven meetings to begin is *three hours after sunset* throughout the year. Sunset colours are typically more brilliant than those of sunrise, because the evening atmosphere contains more particles than in morning. Sometimes, just after sunset, the rare green flash can be seen. This is an optical phenomenon in which a green spot is visible above the Sun, usually for no more than a second – and a *very* rare, magical moment indeed.

Twilight: In the evening, this begins at sunset and ends when the sun reaches six degrees below the horizon. Like the 'blue hour', this 'golden hour', is a favorite with painters and photographers. When the late evening sun is close to the horizon on a sunny day, its light appears warmer and softer: this creates a golden glow, also known as the magical hour, popular with filmmakers. Dusk and twilight are beautiful, evocative words and times: dusk is the darker stage of twilight.

Dusk: Or owl-light, often has a glimmering or imperfect light – occurring at the darkest stage of twilight, or at the very end of astronomical twilight after sunset and just before night. The term *dusk* usually refers to astronomical dusk, or the darkest part of twilight before night actually begins.

Midnight: The moment at which one day ends and the next begins – is twelve o'clock at night. At midnight, the date changes, and the time changes from pm to am. It's no surprise that midnight is the very middle of the night, the word itself stemming from the Old English *mid-niht*, from *mid*, 'among' and *niht*, which appropriately means both 'night' and 'darkness'. In folklore, this witching hour or devil's hour is a time of night associated with supernatural events; a liminal time when creatures such as witches, demons and ghosts were thought to appear and to be at their most powerful – like Macbeth's '*secret, black, and midnight hags*'.

As author Stephen Chamberlain writes, however, the realm of liminality is an abstract concept:

But in that place, that moment or that phase, the order of things is suspended. And yet liminality is a dynamic stage – a tipping point. Whatever lies ahead, when we cross the threshold, the world we know changes. Things are never as they were. Our Ancestors viewed border spaces and times as sacred. In caves and on hilltops, at solstices and equinoxes, the veil between the mundane and supernatural thinned, and cracks opened onto mystical realms. No wonder these liminal conditions, long ago became associated with magic and superstition. There *is* a strangeness about them and it's not what happens when we cross a threshold that molds us, but *how* we react to changes that are to come.

For many of us, however, the evening twilight is the most mysterious of all as it trails a magical cloak across the landscape – and because every landscape has a thousand varying light levels and intensities. There is often a strange iridescent and/or distorted pixilated effect that we refer to as a '*Predator* moment' when the shimmer in the landscape turns to a liquefied gold as it filters through the trees. This golden 'hour' occurs just after sunset, with its length depending on where we are, the time of year and weather conditions.

This strange, luminous light is unlike any other and it can't be replicated because there are natural elements about it that make it quite unique and treasured whenever we experience it. This effect is easily visible, for example, when mountain slopes catch the last rays of the sun, but can also be seen when clouds are affected by light diffusion.

Twilight serves as a liminal time between day and night – where one is 'in the twilight zone, in a liminal nether region of the night'. The title of the television fiction series *The Twilight Zone* makes reference to this, describing it as 'the middle ground between light and shadow, between science and superstition' in one variant of the original series' opening.

The name is from an actual zone observable from space in the place where daylight or shadow advances or retreats about the Earth. Noon and, more often, midnight can also be considered liminal, the first transitioning between morning and afternoon, the latter between days.

Within the yearly cycle, liminal times include Equinoxes when day and night have equal length, and Solstices, when the increase of day or night shifts over to its decrease, marking the cyclical changes of seasons throughout the year. Where the quarter days are held to mark the change in seasons, they are also considered liminal times. New Year's Day, whatever its connection or lack of one to the astrological charts, is also a liminal time.

Nevertheless, this 'golden hour' is all about light. The temperature of the light during this period is, as the name suggests, in the yellow range when it comes into the light spectrum. Without delving too deeply into our chemistry textbooks, light has a spectrum of temperatures that correspond to different colours of light.

During the golden hour, the temperature is in the yellow range, which gives the light a golden hue. When it's warm it creates those ethereal streams of light we see filtering through trees, silhouetting outlines and figures among the lower branches; in an area with lots of tree cover, be mindful of the fact that the light will be diffused all the more.

This is the time that astrophysicist, Chet Raymo describes in *Honey From Stone*, as he searches for the elusive 'green ray' – a momentary burst of colour that can be seen just at the top of the sun as it disappears below the horizon at sunset.

For thirty years I have looked for the green flash ... I became aware of the existence of the green flash in 1965, when I read an article by the astronomer D J K O'Connell of the Vatican Observatory. The effect [he] described was so evanescent, so unexpected, so marvellous, that I have pursued it ever since ... The attraction of the green flash as described by O'Connell was irresistible. But the green flash turned out to be grandly evasive; thirty years later, I am still waiting and watching...

The green flash is *not* an illusion, nor a trick of the retina. At the top margin of the sun's disk – in O'Connell's photograph after photograph – is a brilliant strip of emerald green!

And so here I sit, letting nature tease and tantalise, waiting for a gift of light to be thrown my way. A blink of the eye will be enough to miss it … The flash, if obtained, will be like a signal from out there in the sea of mystery, a signature of the Absolute, a spectral revelation … I have seen my share of lights in the sky. I have seen the aurora borealis and the zodiacal light. I have seen sun dogs and rings around the moon. I have seen double and even triple rainbows. I have seen the midnight sun. But I have not seen the green flash.

I have, however, seen it … once … on a late summer evening when the setting sun had turned the Welsh hills to molten copper. Leaning on a farm gate, staring out over the Teifi Valley as the shadows lengthened and the wooded slopes took on an otherworldly glow of their own – the sun sank below the horizon, leaving behind the precious gift of a millisecond of brilliant emerald green light! These gifts of light in the landscape are fleeting – like the nimbus in heraldry or art it is a solid, luminous circle or beam of light – they can be seen as a liminal experience located in a separate *sacred space*, which occupies a sacred time or dimension. Light is fundamental to the spiritual or mystic experience, and its symbolism pervades the geography of sacred landscapes; it serves as a bridge between interpretation of landscape and the liminal experience.

As Marko Pogačnik explains in *Nature Spirits & Elemental Beings*, originally the earth was shaped by rocks that were left behind in the landscape by glaciers. Through the 'awakening life processes' in the ancestral landscape *after* the glaciers, these different features were chosen by successive cultures who have worshipped at the same places with their differing rituals.

By observing the seasonal light-play over a period of time, we can see the landscape as a complete natural temple area where all types of Otherworldly beings have had their place.

People of the Neolithic culture were the first to utilize natural light in their monuments because they could still clairvoyantly perceive the seasonal light of these particular hills or rocks, which they then developed further to become sacred sites.

In mythology and religion, or esoteric   lore, liminality can include such realms as Purgatory (Catholicism) or Da'at (Qabalah), which – as well as signifying 'between-ness' – some theologians actually deny existing. More conventionally, springs, caves, shores, rivers, volcanic calderas, fords, passes, crossroads, bridges, and marshes are all liminal edges: borders or fault-lines between this and Otherworld. Major transformations occur at crossroads and other liminal places, at least partly because liminality – being so unstable – can pave the way for access to esoteric knowledge or understanding of both sides. Liminality is sacred, alluring, and often dangerous.

Esoterically, liminality is a term used to describe the psychological process of transitioning across boundaries and borders. The term 'limen' comes from the Latin for threshold; it is literally the threshold separating one space from another. The field or wood margin, especially one that has deliberately been left uncultivated, are the strips of land between the field boundary (such as a hedge) and the crop. ...

In agricultural terms, they form a network across the landscape, often linking bigger areas of wildlife habitat, such as woodland or wetland. In esoteric terms, it is a situation where people move from one state of awareness to another; similar to a hypothetical *Stargate* whereby a traversable portal can allow us to access different levels of consciousness and return, retaining the memory of the experience in an altered mindset. As T S Eliot wrote in section five of 'Little Giddings'

We die with the dying:
See, they depart, and we go with them.

We are born with the dead:
See, they return, and bring us with them.

There are a number of stories in folklore narration of those who could only be killed in a liminal space: Lleu is a Welsh hero who appears most prominently in the Fourth Branch of the *Mabinogi.* He is a warrior and magician who could not be killed during the day or night, nor indoors or outdoors, nor riding or walking, nor clothed or naked and is attacked at dusk, while wrapped in a net with one foot on a cauldron and one on a goat!

Likewise, in the Hindu text *Bhagavat Purana,* Vishnu appears in a half-man half-lion form named Narasimha to destroy the demon Hiranyakashipu who has obtained the power never to be killed in day nor night, on the ground nor in the air, with weapon nor by bare hands, in a building nor outside it, by man nor beast. Narasimha kills Hiranyakashipu at dusk, across his lap, with his sharp claws, on the threshold of the palace, and as Narasimha is a god himself, the demon is killed by neither man nor beast. In the *Mahabharata,* Indra promises not to slay Namuci and Vritra with anything wet or dry, nor in the day or in the night, but instead kills them at dusk with foam.

The classic Greek tale of Cupid and Psyche serves as an example of the liminal in myth, exhibited through Psyche's character and the events she experiences. She is always regarded as too beautiful to be human yet not quite a goddess, establishing her uncertain liminal existence. Her marriage to Death in Apuleius's version occupies two classic liminal rites: marriage and death.

Psyche resides in the liminal space of no longer being a maiden yet not quite a wife, as well as living between worlds. Beyond this, her transition to immortality to live with Cupid serves as a liminal rite of passage in which she shifts from mortal to immortal, human to goddess; when Psyche drinks the ambrosia and seals her fate, the rite is completed and the tale ends with a joyous wedding and the birth of the couple's daughter. The characters themselves exist in liminal spaces while experiencing classic rites of passage that necessitate the crossing of thresholds into new realms of existence. *[Intra Limen: An Examination of Liminality in Apuleius' Metamorphoses and Giulio Romano's Sala di Amore e Psiche]*

According to British cultural anthropologist, Victor Turner, the attributes of liminality, or of liminal *personae* ('threshold people') are necessarily ambiguous, because 'one's sense of identity dissolves to some extent, bringing about disorientation, but also the possibility of new perspectives'. Turner, best known for his work on symbols, rituals, and rites of passage, suggests that, 'if liminality is regarded as a time and place of withdrawal from normal modes of social action, it potentially can be seen as a period of scrutiny for central values and axioms of the culture where it occurs - one where normal limits to thought, self-understanding, and behavior are undone. In such situations, the very structure of society [is] temporarily suspended'.

This may also translate into non-magical/spiritual/esoteric areas of our life. For example, we may have noticed that there are certain places or states of being in which we feel different or uncomfortable. Often, these uncomfortable locations can turn out to be liminal spaces. When we find ourselves in liminal spaces, we usually have the feeling of being on the verge of something. Liminal space can be, of course, a *physical* place and there are plenty of examples, according to wellness counsellor, Julia Thomas of Betterhelp:

- Stairwells and elevators are quite clearly in-between spaces or thresholds. Their purpose is to get you from one place to another, and that is why lingering in an empty stairwell or elevator can feel a bit creepy – with liminal space, time can have an

36

impact. An elevator may feel normal during the day, when it's crowded, but certainly not late at night.

- Hallways are another one of those in-between passing zones. During the day, we may see other people passing along the hallway at the same time, making space seem a bit more 'normal'.

- At night, however, it can feel like space has been shut down, and we shouldn't be there. The hallways in our home are familiar but if we're somewhere else, like a hotel or office block, these spaces can feel unfamiliar and a completely unknown environment can seem frightening. Unfamiliar spaces tend to have more liminal qualities than those we see regularly.

- When places lose the function they once had, they can become liminal spaces. Without a light, a lighthouse provides no function and, like non-functioning lighthouses, abandoned buildings are spaces without function. The unsettling aspect occurs because they once performed a role and had people in them. Once abandoned, the lights are always out, and they stand as husks of civilization.

- Most familiar spaces become creepy with the absence of people or light we normally associate with them, simply because our brain has given that space a context and when it doesn't adhere to that context it warns us that something is amiss.

We can see that liminality can be as much a state of the mind as it is a particular place – or an integral part of esoteric practice. Indeed, all the places where we get a sense of liminality are quite usual as far as structures go. It's only in the context we give to them in our minds that they become unusual.

In Old Craft, the liminal veil is what we call the place where a magical transition occurs between the threshold and the place that waits before us. A liminal space may feel confining, but often it takes only minor changes to get through to the next place. Being in a liminal state or place *can* be unsettling and it certainly feels uncomfortable but if we open up to it, it can be the threshold of wonderful new experiences in life.

From the point of view of a traditional British Old Craft witch, this liminality must eventually dissolve, for it is a state of great intensity that cannot exist very long without some sort of structure to stabilize it ... either the individual returns quickly to their surrounding social structure ... or else the witch has been taught how to 'earth' themselves because this is a regular occurrence. Nevertheless, it is important to make sure we earth/ground ourselves after each encounter – just as we would do having completed *any* form of magical/mystical working.

Grounding is the physical connection between the electromagnetic frequencies of the human body with the Earth's. Practicing periodic grounding allows us to focus our mind on the present and learn to feel more balanced and aware. When our mind is unfocused we can feel uneasy, restless, and a state of being uncomfortable – and a chance encounter with a liminal space can leave us feeling this way. Grounding ourselves can help us feel calm, peaceful and centred and one of the simplest methods is to walk barefoot on the ground outside; or sit in a chair with our bare feet on the ground while we have a cup of tea and a sweet biscuit.

Stepping Through the Portal

We shall not cease from exploration
And the end of all our exploring
Will be to arrive where we started
And know the place for the first time.

The simplicity with which we step through the portal depends on the 'witchiness' of the individual. Some have lived their lives with one foot in that other realm, while others struggle unceasingly to gain even the slightest advancement along the Path. Remember that fast learners can adopt a 'know-it-all' state of mind but can soon become lazy. On the other hand, slow learners might be hard workers and will do whatever it takes to find the answer. Fast learners can find things too easy and cut corners, which doesn't always bode well in magic!

'Natural ability' is something that crops up frequently whenever witchcraft is discussed. The definition of 'natural ability' is that with which we are born, whether we call them abilities, talents, gifts or aptitude. We don't know if these magical abilities come about from nature or nurture, but barring something catastrophic happening, these abilities will remain constant throughout our lives. Abilities are not necessarily influenced by education or experiences, whereas magical skills on the other hand can be acquired and perfected.

Although all Coven of the Scales students are introduced to various different practices during the Arcanum foundation course, they are not expected to become proficient in all of them by the end of their studies. Our teaching method enables them to recognize and identify the various cogs in the complex machinery of witchcraft without the need to be fully conversant with all the mechanics and engineering of magical practice. Each lesson is designed as a *starting point* in order to stimulate an interest, and as the studies progress, certain elements will be developed during one-to-one tuition and further guidance.

Discovering liminal spaces can be extremely alarming if we have absolutely no idea what we have encountered but, if we have already been introduced to the concept, we might just be tempted to take a peek before walking away! As noted in Chapter One, the terms gateways, portals and doorways speak for themselves, and as a witch's magical ability is honed these psychic 'gateways' will begin to automatically open – maybe in one, or even several directions simultaneously.

Personal advancement along the Old Craft path depends on an individual's willingness to pass through or stay put, since these gateways open as a result of personal progress serving as an indicator that the time has come to move on and to climb to the next level.

Much of this unexpected psychic activity is a result of being in the right place at the right time. The 'tween times' between day and night are often the usual times to make contact, so try being more receptive at dawn (between night and day) and dusk (between day and night). Other times are at midnight (between one day and the next), any Solstice or Equinox day, at Beltaine and Samhain when the veil between our worlds is very thin so we might want to try that, too. The 'place' is more difficult to define … because our 'Stargate' can be anywhere but at least we will know what it is when we encounter one for the first time.

Victor Turner also introduced us to the idea of *communitas*, the feeling of camaraderie associated among a group experiencing the same liminal experience or rite of initiation within Old Craft. *Communitas* refers to an unstructured state in which all members of a group are equal allowing them to share a common experience, usually through a rite of passage. There is more than one distinction between, shall we say, Coven structure and *communitas*. The most familiar is the difference of secular and sacred: every coven position has something sacred about it. This sacred component is acquired during rites of passage such as experiencing luminality, a vigil or initiation, and through the changing of positions from student to member to Elder.

Communitas is an acute point of Craft community. It takes the Coven to the next level and allows the whole of the membership to share a common experience and the establishing of a group mind. This brings everyone onto an equal level: even if we are higher in position, we have been lower and we know what that means.

Chapter Three: Taking the First Step

A common cosmological theme within the cultures of the Ancient World was the concept that the Otherworld, Underworld or afterlife was entered from this world through portals and these ancient gates *were* often built in stone. Gates and doorways in sacred settings are essentially thresholds and they lend themselves symbolically as entrances into other worlds and alternative realities. These ancient gates represented communications between this world and another, between the living and the dead, and gates protected and guarded voyaging souls as they passaged from one realm to another. Like the false doorways in Egyptian tombs.

In historian J.C. Cooper's 1987 book *An Illustrated Encyclopedia of Traditional Symbols*, the author states that in the Ancient World gates represented '*the protective, sheltering aspect of the Great Mother and were guarded by symbolic animals such as lions, dragons, bulls, dogs or fabulous beasts'.* Thresholds symbolize guarded safe passages between outer profane spaces, to inner, more sacred environs and these boundaries between the natural and the supernatural worlds appear in all genres of storytelling, where heroes pass through as they make their symbolic journey into darkness.

And yet … recent discoveries at Maeshowe on mainland Orkney reveal that in addition to it being one of the earliest examples of a monument being orientated so that the last light of the setting Winter Solstice sun shines along its passage … a new research paper by Jay van der Reijden at the University of the Highlands and Islands

Archaeology Institute made a discovery within the architecture of the 5000-year-old burial chamber which would make it a truly unique monument.

The geometry, shape and design of the 5000-year-old structure demonstrates how the side chambers inside Maeshowe were designed 'upside-down' compared to the stylization featured in the main, or central, chamber. This suggests the side chambers were built as 'inverted netherworlds', specifically designed as conduits for the souls or spirits of the dead to journey to the afterlife.

These new findings have been published (September 2020) in the journal *Archaeological Review*. The paper includes a detailed study of the ancient death chamber's orientation, revealing the design differences between the central and side chambers. Van der Reijden suggests visitors to this monument try to visualize the wall-stones as being like wallpaper: When you repeatedly hang them 'upside down', in certain locations, patterns emerge from the chamber and themes become discernible.

Accounting for these design reversals observed in the side chambers at Maeshowe, van der Reijden explains that they were 'built to be within the netherworld', and that the thick slabs forming the main chamber walls 'acted as membranes, separating this life and the next'. Furthermore, the internal walling material is conceived to 'physically represent the underworld'.

The researcher concludes that these design 'swaps' include the reversal of multiple architectural features which are normally placed on the right-hand side. Meanwhile, in the side chambers of Maeshowe they are situated on the left. She goes on to explain that this was because Neolithic people in Orkney perceived the underworld as a reversed projection of the here and now: just as they saw when looking at their own reflections in rock pools. [*Ancient Origins*]

Van der Reijden also suggests that Maeshowe was not just a stage, or backdrop, for ancient death rituals, but was a *functioning* portal to the otherworld where the scales, ratios and proportions of ancient architecture didn't just represent, but *were* the Underworld.

Since Maeshowe is older than Stonehenge and most of the Egyptian pyramids, it is not unreasonable to assume that other monuments from the Ancient World would perform a similar function. This Mound, aligned with the Winter Solstice, offers us a brief glimpse of how the Neolithic people visualized moving between the worlds.

From the Elder Faith's point of view, however, the Otherworld *we* seek can be best defined as a plane of existence populated by spirit entities, the Ancestors, guardians, numen, *genii loci*, nature sprites, the Fae, discarnate entities, *et al*. And that filmy, iridescent veils that confine them can appear at various times and places throughout the year; a gossamer-fine curtain that wafts in the breeze or night wind and us shows where the veil is at its most vulnerable, inviting us to pass through. The minimal designation for *our* Otherworld is any place inhabited by supernatural beings and itself exhibiting supernatural characteristics.

If we are sensible, our first exploratory attempts at penetrating the veil will be in search of our personal Guardian and the Ancestors, who cast a protective mantle over those of an Old Craft persuasion, and tend to hang around to extract us from the mire whenever we totter too close to the brink. Most Old Crafters find that their Guardian turns up unannounced and when they are least expecting it; those who trudge endless path-workings in pursuit of this elusive being are often doomed to disappointment when their quarry cannot be run to earth! But he/she or it *is* out there, somewhere …

The most common manifestation is the cowled, faceless figure found in religious sculpture across the Romano-Celtic region from Britain to Eastern Europe.

These *hooded entities seem to be relatively common in the reports of monk-like beings that are intimidating, foreboding, and usually downright terrifying. Archetypes of what we dread about the unknown.* While depictions of these mysterious 'Hooded Ones' have been encountered in various places in Europe, the question remains of who these enigmatic cloaked individuals were, and why has the enduring mystery of the faceless figures remained a captivating subject?

Several stone carvings depicting the Hooded Ones, as well as clay statuettes, have been unearthed in Continental Europe and Britain. A famous carving of the Hooded Ones can be found on Hadrian's Wall. They wear a long cloak, covering them from the head to the ankles, making it difficult to see the faces of the carvings. Sometimes the Hooded Ones wear a sword, a fact that gives reason for the speculation as to whether they were guardians. What could they have protected? Although these sculptures resemble those from the Greco-Roman era, the *genius cucullatus* has been considered a figure peculiar to the Celtic cultures of Britain and Gaul.

The most realistic interpretation, however, is Manfred Kielnhofer's unique *Guardians of Time* as a symbol for some greater force that stands above human beings, regardless of the name different people might give to that 'higher power'.

Kielnhofer first designed these sculptures back in 2006 as a kind of statement of belief that human beings are watched over and protected by ancient, god-like forces which occasionally visit the earth. In ancient times, as well as in legendary settings, the *Guardians of Time* are often depicted as cloaked, faceless and hooded figures, wise and powerful ancients that control the destiny of humanity and the threads of time itself. They are creatures of great power, typically not from Earth, and often have a capacity of understanding the

46

universe that dwarfs that of human beings. They are often depicted as mysterious visitors from some far-off place sent to observe, or occasionally intervene in, the progression of humankind. [*The Guardian*]

Kielnhofer has channelled directly into the racial subconscious to come up with these archetypical 'guardians' and this faceless, hooded image is what often creeps into our *conscious* mind when the 'Guardian' chooses to reveal him/her/itself. It was a similar image to that chosen as the logo for Ignotus Press and a short time later an almost identical contemporary statue was discovered in an antiques warehouse in Yorkshire. It was *horrendously* expensive but the decision was made and bearing in mind that 'one should never haggle over a black egg', I presented the credit card … only to discover that the price had been halved in a clearance but the ticket hadn't been altered! The Guardian certainly earned his keep that day …

Other reported encounters, consist of an unseen but comforting/protective presence that has no physical form but nevertheless, was a very distinct presence. From the ancient Chaldeans and Greeks through the 20th-century Western Ritual Magic traditions, the conscious connection with the [Holy] Guardian [Angel] has been one of the most important goals. And, as Aleister Crowley observed:

It is impossible to lay down precise rules by which a man may attain to the knowledge and conversation of his Holy Guardian Angel; for that is the particular secret of each one of us; a secret not to be told or even divined by any other, whatever his grade. It is the Holy of Holies, whereof each man is his own High Priest, and none knoweth the Name of his brother's God, or the Rite that invokes Him. [*Magic Without Tears*]

47

On rarer occasions, the meeting is with an old woman in a traditional cottage/kitchen setting, although the elderly personage is neither warm, nor welcoming. The reception is brusque and often expresses adverse or disapproving comments or judgement ... and yet, there is the feeling of coming away with information imparted and questions answered – despite the fact there was no sense of 'conversation' while being in the Old One's company.

In truth, traditional British Old Craft can be described as an ancestor-cult, since the Ancestors play an integral role in the magical and spiritual workings of the Tradition. They are the intermediaries between humanity and the primal deities who personify our Faceless Goddess and Nameless God, who have little regard for the human race which is hell-bent on destroying each other – and the planet along with them! It is the Ancestors rather than the Old Lass and the Old Lad, who represent our culture, traditions, heritage, lineage and antecedents; who trace the long march of history that our predecessors have taken under the aegis of the Elder Faith.

When those of a particular Tradition pass beyond the veil, their spiritual essence merges with the divine spirit of the Whole, which in turn gives traditional witchcraft the continuing power to endure – even past its own time and place in history. It therefore remains the duty of an Old Craft practitioner to ensure that the soul of any newly deceased can successfully join the Ancestors and keep adding to the strength of the Elder Faith, which, in many instances may already have endured for hundreds – if not thousands of years. If when living, we cannot acknowledge and respect the Ancestors of traditional British Old Craft to which we *claim* to belong, then we will contribute nothing to the Whole when we die.

The honouring of the dead and venerating their memory is a common root of all belief, with many cultures telling that the dead live on in another dimension, continuing to affect the lives of subsequent generations.

This concept of spirit-ancestors is an extremely ancient one, especially when it involves dealing with deceased members of a particular people or tribe, and is still widely observed in Japanese Shinto, Chinese Confucianism and among the Australian Aboriginal and Native American peoples.

In the West, we know from the remains of the numerous prehistoric earthworks that the indigenous people of the British Isles and later the Celts honoured their ancestors; and interaction with these spirit-ancestors as an invisible but powerful presence is a constant feature of the Elder Faith, with the Ancestors remaining important members of the Tradition of those they have left behind. In general, they are seen as Elders, treated and referred to in much the same way as the most senior of living Elders of a coven or magical group, with additional mystical and magical powers.

We may first encounter them as a shadowy presence on the periphery of our vision when we cast the *Samhain* Compass but they are unable to enter because of the magical boundary. If and when we decide the time has come to meet them face to face, then our *Samhain* rites must be performed *sans* circle, so that there is no barrier between us and them. We have known experienced Crafters cast the Compass when undergoing an important liminal ritual, thereby excluding the Ancestors from the proceedings … and themselves from being on the receiving end of any communication they may wish to impart from Otherworld.

It is possible that our Guardian *may* be one of the Ancestors at a more recent level along the 'ancestral way' – similar to the *bodhisattva* (Buddhism) who foregoes entrance into Nirvana in order to remain in the world as long as there are those who need to be guarded and guided. Sometimes they are identified with the Mighty Dead, the Watchers or the Old Ones, who gave magical knowledge to mankind, rather than merely family or tribal dead. Or, even more ambiguously 'those who have gone before' – their magical essence distilled into the universal or racial subconscious at different levels.

Reverence for Craft Ancestors is part of the ethic of respect for those who have preceded us in life, and their continued presence on the periphery of our consciousness means that they are always with us. And, because traditional witchcraft is essentially a practical thing, the Ancestors are also called upon to help find solutions to magical problems through divination, path-working and spell-casting.

There is an historical precedence for these beliefs and with apologies to Kenneth Grant for the paraphrasing from *Hecate's Fountain* …

> *It may be asked, why then do we not abandon these ancient customs in favour of more contemporary observances? The answer is that the traditional witch and magical practitioner understands that contact with these old energies may be established more completely through customs that are so ancient that they have had time to firmly entrench themselves in the vast storehouse of the racial subconsciousness. To such offerings and oblations the Forces respond swiftly and with incalculable fullness, whereas newly devised rites and rituals possess no link with those elements in the psyche to which they can appeal - and lead, only too often, away from the goal. Contemporary Wicca has evolved too recently to serve as a direct conduit. For the Old Ones, such lines of communication are dead. The Old Craft witch, therefore, uses the more direct paths which long ages have mapped out in the shadowlands of the subconsciousness.*

Be warned, however, that these Otherworld beings are not particularly well-disposed towards us and are swift to anger over what they may see as an act of *lèse-majesté* against their person, or the Tradition. It's not unusual for one of the Coven's Elders to observe that one of the members will shortly 'come a cropper' for some serious breach of Craft etiquette because the Ancestors have long memories – and are nothing if not a tad vindictive when it suits them. We use 'come a cropper' to mean that a person has been struck by some momentous and unexpected misfortune, but it derives from the hunting field, where it originally meant a heavy fall from a horse. And anything that is considered 'god given' – something that is so extraordinary that it could only have come from a higher power – can just as quickly be taken away.

Although students are made aware of the existence of personal Guardians, the Ancestors and liminal spaces, it would be inadvisable for them to go searching haphazardly for them without sufficient experience to understand *what* it is they may encounter in their quest. Otherworld is densely populated with all manner of psychic entities and, whereas the Guardian and the Ancestors are *not ill-disposed* towards the seeker, the same cannot be said of other denizens of this realm – many of whom can be downright maleficent.

The would-be witch is instructed in various methods of psychic protection that serves to act as a barrier against anonymous manifestations that may be attracted to the energy released when we begin flexing our psychic muscles on a very lowly level. At this stage of our magical development, the attacks may be no more than the equivalent of 'astral fleas' and a prompt treatment of magical Frontline will quickly sort the problem out! A seasonal protective spell for our home will usually be sufficient to keep everyone and everything in it safe, providing our amulets and witch-balls are recharged at the same time.

Remember that no amount of occult shop clutter will keep you safe if the appropriate charms and protective spells have not been cast periodically to form a magical

51

barrier. Nevertheless, there comes a time when we can be hampered by too much protection and these psychic barriers can create a resistance, which blocks the flow of energy that distorts our perception.

This often occurs when practitioners have been pursuing an eclectic form of magical study and have called down an assortment of cross-cultural entities to act as their protector(s). This can lead to one cancelling another out, or a confusing, multi-layering of conflicting energies. These psychic barriers lead to the creation of magical blind spots; because these psychological patterns operate outside conscious awareness. Therefore, as a consequence when an individual continually resists life-learning messages by generating further psychic barriers, they merely create a whole range of negative emotions, which *nothing* can penetrate. Psychic barriers are indiscriminate and do not differentiate between positive and negative messages – having been in place for a very long time.

On the positive side, beginners are often protected by an unseen, guiding hand when they are starting to explore unfamiliar astral pathways and suddenly confront some strange and impenetrable barrier. It can be a fear from our subconscious – like a gigantic spider; or some other terrifying creature. Whatever … the pathway is blocked and we cannot pass. Because we are beginners, we decide that discretion is definitely the better part of valour and we turn back. The next time we travel that path there is nothing stopping us from carrying on and so we proceed – but with a certain degree of wariness.

What would have happened if we'd pressed on regardless the first time? A physical reaction, perhaps, or the scenario might have blown up into nightmare proportions. Either way, it would have been a terrifying experience. If we are told 'the way is shut' then we must learn to take heed and obey because we *will* encounter these warnings throughout our magical career.

I recall one instance where I came across a well-known liminal place on a local track through an established conifer forest. A guest, who was also an Elder of the Coven wanted to walk among the trees, despite the unwelcoming ambience of the place. A short distance from the entrance, the dog and I got the same feeling at the same time … that we were not welcome in the forest and we turned back.

Undeterred, the guest tramped on, making a devil of a racket; eventually, the undergrowth closed in around him and he was forced to retreat. He emerged further along the track but before he could physically exit the wood, he was picked up bodily and given 'the bum's rush' … that is, a forcible and swift ejection from the place!

We may consider ourselves to be fully-fledged members of the pagan community but this is no guarantee that Otherworld is going to recognize or honour those credentials. We always enter this realm under sufferance and if the signs aren't welcoming then it might be in our best interests to retreat; especially if we have surrounded ourselves with a powerful protective aura that the denizens of Otherworld may be finding offensive. Should we enter Otherworld with a strong, protective shield in place, it can hardly be considered good manners if *we* are giving off 'keep away' vibes when we enter their territory!

Superstition and the established religions would like everyone to bask in the spiritual certainty that there was a personal guardian angel watching over each and every one of us from birth to the grave, but in reality, the answer is not so simple. These 'guardians' may watch over mankind in order to single out the 'promising students' in terms of spiritual development, but as each individual succumbs to the lure of earthly pursuits and material pleasures, so the Guardians withdraw to concentrate their energies on those who stay the course.

This particular kind of cosmic bonding was *never* an option for all. It was the growing power of the incoming priesthoods that overthrew the early priest-astronomers, and who promised eternal and everlasting life to the common man. It might have been Karl Marx who coined the phrase that religion was the opium of the people, but he was not the first to have realised this – the concept was already being exploited by the Osirian priesthood as early as Dynasty VI in ancient Egypt! The elitist Old Order had been swept away and, in the place of direct communication with the ancestral entities, there was an ancient equivalent of happy-clappy evangelism that promised everyone would be welcomed into the embrace of the Osirian gods in the afterlife.

The Ancestors, of course, are *not* individuals blessed with everlasting life but they are a power-source of distilled energy from all the 'souls' of our Tradition who have gone before. They are the essence of the six million years that humans have been on the planet; the ones most closely related to us date back to sometime between 200,000 and 300,000 years ago.

Archaeologists working in Morocco found a jawbone that dates to this era. It also matched similar bones found in other regions; some evidence indicates that these humans lived in parts of modern-day Greece, Europe and Israel. Archaeologists in Israel found a *homo sapien* jawbone that was more than 175,000 years old, which makes it the oldest bone found on the continent, and some of the humans who lived in Ethiopia at that time were using ritual when burying their dead.

These were the ancestors of Old Europe who constructed Gobekli Tepe – possibly the world's oldest temple – whose megaliths predate Stonehenge by some 6,000 years. Nor forgetting Newgrange in Ireland, Gavrinis in Brittany and Maeshow in Orkney with their mid-winter alignments that enshrine Neolithic beliefs as powerful and as complex as those of the ancient

Egyptians. Or the ancestral [racial] memory whose roots dig even deeper into the past of the French and Iberian phenomenon of Upper Palaeolithic cave art, whose people harnessed what we call altered states of consciousness that made such image-making possible at *Les Trois Frères*, Lascaux and Altamira.

> To my way of thinking, there is no greater archaeological enigma than the subterranean art of Upper Palaeolithic western Europe. Anyone who has crouched and crawled underground along a narrow, absolutely dark passage for more than a kilometre, slid along mud banks and waded through dark lakes and hidden rivers to be confronted at the end of such a hazardous journey, by a painting of an extinct woolly mammoth or a powerful, hunched bison will never be quite the same again. Muddied and exhausted, the explorer will be gazing at the limitless *terra incognita* of the human mind. [David Lewis-Williams, *The Mind in the Cave*]

This ancestral memory in psychological terms, refers to the subconscious memory of events in the history of the human race (or occasionally one's own race) which, it is suggested, is transmitted genetically. Whether called genetic, ancestral or racial memory – intuitional or congenital gifts, the concept of a genetic transmission of sophisticated knowledge well beyond instincts, is necessary to explain how esoteric practitioners can 'know' things they never learned. Carl Jung used the term 'collective unconscious' to define his even broader concept of inherited traits, intuitions and collective wisdom of the past.

It is here, as we stand on the threshold of Otherworld that we begin to realize what a complex and dangerous domain we are attempting to enter. We are leaving behind the secure and structured sphere of the Compass and

55

venturing out into the great unknown. Nevertheless, Otherworld plays an intrinsic and inseparable part in the Elder Faith because this is where the inner secrets of our magical learning are played out. The Ancestors, who have probably been a filmy shadow-play on the periphery of our vision, now become more real and substantial; the seasonal rites of the Compass now become unmistakable elements of sabbatic witchcraft; and the rites of passage (namely Initiation) stamp their indelible mark on us. In *The Eye in the Triangle*, Israel Regardie describes this process in these words:

> All we can say honestly and simply is that the awakening comes. There is no certain method, no stereotyped set of stimuli or patterns, no standard set of responses. But when it is there, when it does come, the individual is never the same. It is rather like being brought to the Light, in the ritualistic sense, except that this is no ritual. It occurs in the most natural, and, in one sense, the most unsought way.

But this descent into the Mysteries does not confer automatic insight into the 'powers that be'.

> *These are the experiences and events which occur to every aspirant when initiation forces the realisation upon him, through the activation of the latent contents* of his own psyche, that 'all is sorrow'. In fact, the *existential criterion or hall-marks of successful initiation is the occurrence of these or similar experiences.*

Here we find that direct contact with Otherworld following Initiation does *not* bring an inner peace and contentment ... in fact, the reverse is true. The Initiate is overwhelmed by a sense of futility and desolation; the 'innocence' of the pre-initiatory state cannot be regained, and the way ahead is uncertain and dangerous.

Again, the difference between science, theology and mysticism is that the true witch is always willing to risk his or her life and sanity in pushing the boundaries of the mystical experience in pursuit of 'truth'. In order to understand something of the process and ethos of mystical Initiation, we have to bear in mind that the aim is to help produce a spiritually self-conscious and self-sufficient individual. In order to achieve this, the individual has to be a well-equipped 'all-rounder', not just someone with highly developed 'occult' powers. In recent years, so much has been made of the issue of Initiation into the Mysteries that people tend to forget about the very necessary and very extended prior training, the latter in itself being no guarantee of success for the individual. Successful accomplishment of mystical advancement, however, offers a chance to walk between the worlds and attain, in esoteric terms – 'conversation with the Holy Guardian Angel'.

Once the Initiate has stepped through the portal, there is no going back and it alters the perspective on almost everything that we once held to be of worth and consequence. Even family and friends assume a lesser degree of importance when compared with the quest upon which we have embarked. This is why the first steps on the Path should never be taken lightly or without due thought about the consequences. We must accept that those we care about cannot lay claim to 'everlasting life' whether it be a Christian or pagan afterlife, and that we may never again cross paths with those we've considered to be our soul-mates.

There can be no re-tracing of our steps once we have stepped through the Gate.

Traditional British Old Craft is not for the faint-hearted. Nevertheless, if we fail to grasp the importance or appreciate the opportunity at its full value, we will have missed the supreme chance of our spiritual life and the gateways (or stargates) to Otherworld will be shut to us, at best for this lifetime, at worst – forever.

Parting the Veil

It cannot be emphasised strongly enough, that we are *not* claiming traditional British Old Craft's practices go back to the Stone Age. It was wild flights of fancy such as this that led to the derisive dismissal of Margaret Murray's theory that witches were members of a huge secret society preserving a prehistoric fertility cult through the centuries. Ironically, she was a wholehearted sceptic and rationalist, who wanted to strip away every notion of the paranormal or supernatural from the concept of witchcraft ... and by doing this she rendered her version of historical witchcraft sterile.

Needless to say, her detractors were academics and historians who had never seen the inside of a witch's Circle either ... which also rendered many of their own observations invalid. A true Old Craft witch, however, *can* read between the lines of Murray's writings and find where her omissions and 'judicious' editing of magical references rendered the text nonsensical – and, discover where certain *facts* survived her selection process because she has not realized that they were referring to magical stuff! There are numerous isolated passages within the text of *The Witch-Cult in Western Europe,* that contain valid Old Craft information not found in any other books on the subject and not generally known outside Craft.

This may well explain why her methodology was so unsafe once she stepped outside the boundaries of her own speciality – Egyptology – and time – the 1920s and 30s. Because racial memory, simply put, is complex; abilities and actual sophisticated knowledge inherited along with other more typical and commonly accepted physical and behavioural characteristics *is* genetic. In occult practitioners, this esoteric 'chip' comes factory installed. For example: Brian Butterworth, in his 1999 book, *What Counts: How Every Brain is Hardwired for Math*, points out that babies have many specialized innate abilities, including numerical ones that he attributes to a 'number module' encoded in the human genome from ancestors some 30,000 years ago!

But in contemporary jargon, many an Old Craft witch apparently comes already programmed with a vast amount of innate skill and knowledge in his or her area of expertise – factory-installed 'software' one might say – which accounts for the extraordinary abilities over which the witch innately shows mastery in the face of often massive cognitive and/or other learning handicaps. In short, certain people may show explosive and sometimes prodigious Craft ability, which often lies dormant until released by a process of recognition or awakening.

It's hardly surprising that the majority of today's clinical psychologists regard Carl Jung as a mystic because he believed humans have a soul and that we are all connected at a deep, shrouded level of the mind he termed the 'collective unconscious'. This arose from a common repository of mankind's figures, narratives, and symbols which share a great deal of commonality throughout the ages and across different cultures. According to Jung, the human collective unconscious [racial memory] is populated by instincts, as well as by archetypes: universal symbols such as The Great Mother, the Wise Old Man, the Shadow, the Tower, Water, and the Tree of Life.

He opined that the collective unconscious had profound influence on the lives of certain individuals, who lived out its symbols and clothed them in meaning through their experiences … which is why his work is generally understood (if not totally accepted) by serious witches and occultists who feel most attuned to his ideas. In reading Jung, we may just feel intuitively that much of what he offered was right in terms of our own experiences because he was one of the few psychologists for whom spiritual elements in mankind were as important as other faculties.

Chapter Four: The Enchanted Realm

As we have seen, Otherworld can best be defined as a plane of existence populated by spirit entities besides the Ancestors. What we must never lose sight of is the fact that these energies/entities can be helpful or harmful, and should be treated with the greatest respect and caution. These are cosmic energies on a very low level but they are far more powerful than can ever be imagined and as such can destroy us if treated in a cavalier manner.

To return to Bob Clay-Egerton's analogy that a trained pearl or sponge diver can reach very much greater depths, for longer periods, than can the untrained diver – who can, nevertheless, reach greater depths in safety than a non-swimmer. Once we have passed through the luminal gateways on a regular basis, we can begin to penetrate further into Otherworld and meet the denizens that populate every level of this strange realm …

Guardian spirits of place are those who inhabit the locale of tomb, burial mound and barrow, and were, no doubt, originally evoked by the priests or tribal shamans as protectors – to prevent outsiders making use of the site's energies. Sacred sites become sacred by a dedicated usage while other places may have been consecrated for a specific use.

Rituals held in the past would probably have been dedicated to the cult of the Ancestors and possibly death/rebirth/ regeneration, when aligned with the Winter Solstice. It seems unlikely that such sites would have been visited for anything other than the rites for which they were intended. In *Needles of Stone*, dowser Tom Graves cites the group of students who 'acquired' a *grimoire* and decided to perform a magical working on top of an ancient earth barrow at night – for fun! Whatever happened spooked the group so badly that they panicked and ran.

According to Graves, it was impossible to get an exact description of what suddenly appeared on top of the barrow, as its appearance was slightly different for each of the students involved. As any seasoned witch would have realized, however, this is a characteristic of 'guardians' and many other kinds of Otherworld entities.

For days afterwards the students were plagued by the fear of being stalked, some even requiring psychiatric counselling before they were able to overcome the fear of being followed. This is merely an ancient safety valve to stop inexperienced or foolish people from coming into contact with forces they cannot control or understand.

Or, in the words of Madame Arcati from Noël Coward's *Blithe Spirit*: 'If you were foolish enough to tamper with the unseen for paltry motives and in a spirit of ribaldry, whatever has happened to you is your own fault and, to coin a phrase, as far as I'm concerned you can stew in your own juice!'

In *The Secret Country*, Janet and Colin Bord recorded the evidence of so many ancient sites that appear to be associated with the manipulation and storage of power or energy. Some, including Tom Lethbridge, have experienced shocks when touching these old standing stones that imply some megaliths carry a current of some kind. Not all people can feel them, and they are not always present, suggesting the ebb and flow of a current – possibly a subterranean stream or river – and as most stone circles are now incomplete, perhaps something *has* gone from them.

The late Guy Underwood, through his dowsing abilities, discovered a complex system of water lines, which he identified as a geodetic system. He felt strongly that these geodetic lines provided a clue to the religion of our pre-history, because his investigations showed that all ancient structures mark significant geodetic features. He also felt that an unknown force was involved, the characteristics of which he outlined in his book, *The Pattern of the Past*, where he suggests it may be 'an unrecognized effect of some already established force, such as magnetism or gravity'.

It has long been believed that prehistoric monuments, especially stone circles, were originally used as astronomical calculators and possibly for rituals of some kind. The Bords' speculate that at least part of their function involved energetic dancing designed to generate power, which was then reabsorbed back into the stones – with echoes down to the present day in the witchcraft rituals sometimes performed at these sites. Tom Lethbridge's interpretation of the possible use of stone circles is worth quoting:

Apparently the belief that power could be obtained by stepping up the current in human bodies is very old indeed. The stone circles, which are usually thought to be temples of some kind, are most probably places where violent dancing in a ring took place to engender power, much in the same way as in electricity, a moving coil generates power. The stones were probably put there with the idea of containing the power once it had been generated [*Witches: Investigating an Ancient Religion*]

There is some indication that a similar effect might be produced by a line of dancers weaving in and out of the stones of a circle, perhaps holding hands in order to connect their bodies together in a chain. By these movements, they would cut through the lines of magnetic flow, and so step up the voltage. The rapid movement of a line of dancers in and out among the stones could have resulted in the generation of an energy that the quartz

63

stones (frequently to be found in stone circles), would store or conduct into the earth. Alternatively, the dance could have produced alterations in the electrical brain waves of the dancers, possibly enabling them to apprehend other levels of consciousness so integral to sabbatic witchcraft.

If prehistoric monuments were used for this type of ritual purpose, it wouldn't be surprising if a powerful simulacrum or thought-form manifested as a 'guardian' as a result. 'It is also questionable whether prehistoric burial structures, especially the more complex megalithic tombs, were built primarily to house the dead, or whether they may also have had other more obscure uses.

The possibility that megalithic tombs may have had other functions, of which traces no longer remain, should not be discarded. The small chambers within the tombs could have been used for the performance of esoteric rituals or ceremonies, or by those seeking mystic experiences.' [*The Secret Country*]

Throughout history, to disturb an ancient site or remove an old stone was to invite disaster, and there are many instances that give warnings to would-be desecrators and others telling what befell those who disregarded the warnings. As Tom Graves observes in *Needles of Stone*:

There is another type of 'activation of ancient celtic (*sic*) sites by magicians' which does seem to be important in any study of haunting, even though it doesn't seem to affect the 'colouring' of the energies: and that is the creation and activation of what my magician friends call 'guardians'. Fortunately these are rare, for the various reports I've had of them suggests that they can be extremely dangerous …[with] the storage of a protective function or idea in that it has a limited amount of choice and intelligence both in the choice of form in which it appears, and the movements

64

and effects it can have … It may be that a fair number of the legends of 'divine retribution' against barrow-robbers and the like are due to these elemental 'guardians': no matter how crazy it may sound, these 'active images' do have a real force, and are not to be taken lightly.

In classical Roman religion, a **genius loci** (plural *genii locorum*) was the protective spirit of a place or location. It was often depicted in religious iconography as a figure holding attributes such as a *patera* (libation bowl) cornucopia, or a snake. In contemporary usage, *genius loci* usually refers to a location's distinctive atmosphere, or a 'spirit of the place', rather than necessarily a guardian spirit. Every place has its own unique qualities, not only in terms of its physical makeup, but of how it is perceived in the prevailing character or ambience.

Those key points are reflected in the general pagan view of the 'spirit' of a place. The contemporary viewpoint is that places are just commodities, to be bought and sold like any other commodity; but in the pagan view, probably best typified by that of the Native American people, places can have a sacredness, a spiritual importance, that seems to bear no relation to the more physical characteristics of the place.

Beyond these, however, there are other sets of characteristics more of the forces of Nature than of man, but which also have recognizable functions and forms, according to Tom Graves. Archetypes that arise from an interaction between man and Nature, or within and of Nature itself, metamorphosing as a *genius loci* in the landscape, together with its flora and fauna.

Similarly, **numen** is a spiritual force or influence often identified with a natural object, phenomenon, or place - filled with or characterized by a sense of a supernatural presence. Since the early 20th century, *numen* has sometimes been treated in the history of religion as a pre-animistic phase; that is, a belief system inherited from an earlier time. *Numen* is also used by sociologists to refer to the idea of magical power residing in an object, particularly when writing about ideas in the western tradition. Or, as Christopher Tilley observes in *A Phenomenology of Landscape:*

> There is an art of moving in the landscape, a right way to move around in it and approach places and monuments. Part of the sense of place is the action of approaching it from the 'right' direction.' The method of approach is governed by a combination of place and time – both seasonal and social – while the 'art' is the simultaneous practice of meditation and ritualized operation. 'Flashes of memory, so to speak, illuminate the occasion and bestows an instinctive grasp of how to behave within a ritual or sacred landscape, and to recognize the type of magical energy to be encountered there.

The expression *Numen inest* appears in Ovid's *Fasti* and has been translated as 'There is a spirit here'. The supposition is that a *numinous presence* in the natural world is supposed in the earliest layers of Italic religion, as an 'animistic' element left over in historical Roman religion.

Nature spirits are composed of etheric matter and are the forces or personifications of the forces of nature and the most familiar forms are the nymphs of Greek mythology, typically identified with natural features such as mountains (*oreads*), trees and flowers (*dryads* and *meliae*), springs, rivers and lakes (*naiads*) or the sea (*nereids*), or as part of the divine retinue of a comparable god such as Apollo, Dionysos or Pan, or goddesses, such as Artemis, who was known as the tutelary deity of all nymphs.

These nymphs were also spirits invariably bound to places, not unlike the Latin *genius loci* and presided over various natural phenomena – from springs, to clouds, trees, caverns, meadows, and beaches. They were responsible for the care of the plants and animals of their domain and as such were closely associated with the Olympian gods of nature, while some, like the *hamadryad* (oak-tree dryads) were bound to the life-force of a particular tree.

Often nymphs tended to frequent areas distant from humans but could be encountered by lone travellers outside the village, where their music might be heard, and the traveller could spy on their dancing or bathing in a stream or pool, either during the noon heat or in the middle of the night. They might appear in a whirlwind.

Such encounters could be fraught with danger, bringing dumbness, besotted infatuation, madness or stroke to the unfortunate human. Since medieval times, nymphs are sometimes popularly associated or even confused with faeries, in that they were unpredictable, a little scary: some were downright dangerous.

Elementals are composed of earth, air, fire and water – and are described in occult and alchemical works from around the time of the European Renaissance, and particularly elaborated in the 16th-century works of Paracelsus. In the Western tradition, the first book to bring together all the different species of elementals into one coordinated system and which described their unique characteristics, was *About Nymphs, Sylphs, Pygmies and Salamanders and Other Spirits*.

Here Paracelsus opined that elemental spirits were equal to human souls in the value of their evolutionary development. Tom Graves, however, maintains that nature spirits are elementals similar to the 'barrow-guardians' we looked at earlier: but they are natural rather than artificially created. Another way of looking at them is to say they are, like the guardians – constructs – but constructed by nature rather than by man.

> Like the barrow-guardians, these nature-spirits [elementals] seem to be limited in their movements and the scope of their activity, and to have little individual intelligence; but the group-intelligence is enormous, and is traditionally represented by the nature-god Pan. Pan is unlimited in movement or scope of action – in the original Greek he is literally 'everywhere' – and his form, half animal, half human, represents the marrying of the forces of nature with a kind of intellect. The apparent form, again, is symbolic, rather than representational of any physical entity. The elemental archetype is more often sensed than seen; and it's likely, as one of the community explained, that it is only seen when it 'wants' to be seen. [*Needles of Stone*]

It is obvious that there is a tremendous amount of mythical overlay and cross-dressing when it comes to identifying and understanding these different characteristics. If we see this vast range of 'spirits' not as entities with fixed anthropomorphic forms but as abstract energy whose appearance varies according to the form in which we want or expect to see them.

These energy-forms have been with us from the time humans first emerged from their cave. Over time, they have revealed themselves as anything that made sense to primitive humans. The energies remained the same and the representation remains the same; but the appearances changes to match the spirit of the time.

68

Faere Folk and People of the Hollow Mounds - also *fay*, *fae*, *fey* or *faerie* [Old French] – are a type of mythical being or legendary creature found in the folklore of multiple European cultures (including Celtic, Slavic, German, English, and French folklore), a form of spirit, often described as metaphysical, supernatural, or preternatural.

Myths and stories about faeries do not have a single origin, but are rather a collection of folk beliefs from disparate sources. Various folk theories about the origins of faeries include casting them as either demoted angels or demons in a Christian tradition; as deities in pagan belief systems; as spirits of the dead; as prehistoric precursors to humans, or as spirits of nature.

The label of *faerie* has at times applied only to specific magical creatures with human appearance, magical powers, and a penchant for trickery. At other times it has been used to describe any magical creature, such as goblins and gnomes. *Faerie* has at times been used as an adjective, with a meaning equivalent to 'enchanted' or 'magical'. It is also used as a name for the place these beings come from: the land of Faere Folk.

- **England**

Faerie entities, in their restricted sense, are unique in English folklore, though these non-human spirits abound Celtic and Germanic folk beliefs. Most of us think of the fae as tiny creatures, flitting about on gossamer wings, waving a magic wand (as in Disney's *Fantasia*), but history and folklore tell a different tale.

Even when belief in faeries was common, most people didn't like to mention them by name and so referred to them by other names: the 'Little People' or the 'Hidden People'. The oldest faeries on record in England were first described by the historian Gervase of Tilbury in the 13th century.

It was during the Elizabethan Age, however, when William Shakespeare had popularised faeries in English folklore, in his play *Midsummer Night's Dream*, with the characters Oberon, Titania and Puck (Robin Goodfellow). Earlier than Shakespeare, Chaucer (1342-1400) mentioned that the land of Britain was filled with faeries before the time of King Arthur.

In the Arthurian legends, faerie figures appeared in abundance. Morgana, Arthur's half-sister, seemed to be a great sorceress and healer, was often called Morgan le Fay. Then there was the Lady of the Lake, and not forgetting Arthur's wife, Guinevere, or Gwenhwyfar in the Welsh tradition, who also appeared to be part faerie. Many knights were either born from faeries or they took female faeries as their lovers, and even good old Merlin was only part mortal.

Then we discover that these images of the Faere Folk are not the only kind. There were all sorts in faerie tales and folklore. Some are benign, while others are malignant and hostile to mortals. Some were seen as fair, while others were considered ugly and monstrous to look upon. They came in all shapes and sizes – so there is really no clear definition of what faeries may look like.

Different types of fae may also have different types of magical powers. In his story *The Dymchurch Flit* Rudyard Kipling ascribes the faeries' flight to the ill-will generated by religious dissension and the sense that they were no longer welcome and did not belong: '*Fair or foul, we must flit out o' this, for Merry England's done with, an' we're reckoned among the Images*'.

- **Wales**

Welsh-born writer Arthur Machen (1863-1947) is best known for his Gothic horror novels, but beyond this, he believed that the humdrum visible world conceals a more mysterious and strange reality. Faerie-lore was just one element of his wide reading that he combined into this vision, acknowledging the rational explanations for faerie belief (*Tylwyth Teg*) and for the origins of faeries (later set out in detail by Lewis Spence in *British Fairy Origins* of 1946):

I am well aware, of course, of the various explanations of the fairy mythology; the fairies are the gods of the heathen come down into the world: Diana becomes Titania. Or the fairies are a fantasy on the small dark people who dwelt in the land before the coming of the Celts; or they are elementals - spirits of the four elements: there are all these accounts, and for all I know, may be true, each in its measure.

Machen dismissed the more intangible of these scientific interpretations, but he was strongly attracted by the idea of 'little people' who still survived in out of the way places, although he saw them as being something far more primitive and alien. In *The Novel of the Black Seal* (1895) one character expands upon this:

I was especially drawn to consider the stories of the fairies, the good folk of the Celtic races. Just as our remote ancestors called the dreaded beings 'fair' and 'good' precisely because they dreaded them, so they had dressed them up in charming forms, knowing the truth to be the reverse. Literature too had gone early to work, and had lent a powerful hand in the transformation, so that the playful elves of Shakespeare are already far removed from the true original and the real horror is disguised in a form of prankish mischief.

In Machen's writing, the word 'faerie' seems to have three distinct, but layered or related, meanings. This is well-illustrated by sampling its usage in his novels, especially the 1922s *The Secret Glory:*

Faery' can imply something merely curious, unusual and lovely. This may be applied to things as trivial as a young couple in awe as they discover London, to the metropolis that the same couple uncover for the first time, or to a salad in a French restaurant; but it also, more poetically, describes a snowbound scene as a 'white fairyland', and he sees in a sunset sky 'golden lances [that] glittered in a field of faerie green' as well as 'the green of the faery seas'. This usage shades imperceptibly into a sense of something mysterious, magical and beautiful, as in 'the faery hills and woods and valleys of the West'. More specifically, those seas reappear in a reference to 'ships of the saints, without oar or sail, afloat on the faery sea, seeking the Glassy Isle' - that is, the isle of Avalon, *Ynys Wytrin* at Glastonbury; and the 'faery apple-garths in Avalon.

Touring Wales in late Victorian times, Professor John Rhys was several times told that faeries were no longer encountered in the countryside. They had been seen 'daily by shepherds in the age of faith gone by, in the 'faerie days'– but no more. They have been deliberately exorcised: it was explained to John Rhys that they did not appear as in a 'former age' because they had been cast out (*ffrymu*) for a period of centuries and would not be back during 'our time'.

It is interesting that this ejection, albeit long, was considered a temporary state - a reason for some to be hopeful, perhaps … And, an explanation as to why the Faere Folk have no great love for the close proximity of humans.

- **Ireland**

Tuatha Dé Danann are a race of supernaturally-gifted people in Irish mythology. They are thought to represent the main deities of pre-Christian Ireland and many of the Irish modern tales of the Tuatha Dé Danann refer to these beings as faeries, though in more ancient times they were regarded as divine. Spoken of as having come from islands in the north of the world or, in other sources, from the sky.

After being defeated in a series of battles with other Otherworldly beings, and then by the ancestors of the current Irish people, they were said to have withdrawn to the *sídhe* (fairy mounds), where they lived on in popular imagination as 'faeries'. They are associated with several Otherworld realms including *Mag Mell* (the Pleasant Plain), *Emain Ablach* (the place of apples), and *Tír na nÓg* (the Land of Youth).

Similarly, the *aos sí* is the Irish term for a supernatural race in Irish, comparable to faeries or elves. Again, they are variously said to be ancestors, the spirits of nature, or old goddesses and gods. A common theme found among the Celtic nations describes a race of people who had been driven out by invading humans.

In old Celtic fairy lore, the *aos sí* (people of the fairy mounds) are immortals living in the ancient barrows and cairns. The Irish banshee (Irish Gaelic *bean sí* which means 'woman of the fairy mound') is sometimes described as a ghost

- **Scotland**

In Scottish folklore, faeries are divided into the *Seelie Court* (more beneficently inclined, but still dangerous), and the *Unseelie Court* (more malicious). While faeries of the *Seelie Court* enjoyed playing generally harmless pranks on humans, those of the *Unseelie Court* often brought harm to humans for entertainment. Both could be dangerous to humans if offended. In the 1691 *The Secret Commonwealth of Elves, Fauns and Fairies*, Reverend Robert Kirk, minister of the Parish of Aberfoyle, Stirling, Scotland, wrote:

73

These *Siths* or Fairies they call *Sleagh Maith* or the Good People ... are said to be of middle nature between Man and Angel, as were Daemons thought to be of old; of intelligent fluidous Spirits, and light changeable bodies (lyke those called Astral) somewhat of the nature of a condensed cloud, and best seen in twilight. These bodies be so pliable through the sublety of Spirits that agitate them, that they can make them appear or disappear at pleasure.

In the Middle Ages, faeries feature in the Border ballads and in medieval romance. Traditionally they were as tall as humans, but they could also be very tiny; like their human counterparts, they spent their time hunting, hawking and feasting. Stories of the period also told of the 'Faerie Rade', when they rode in procession on white horses, hung with silver bells. The story of Scotland's last Fairy Rade was told by the Scottish writer, Hugh Miller, more than 100 years ago.

A herd-boy and his sister saw a procession of glittering strangers riding through a hamlet near Glen Eathie. As the last rider passed by, the boy asked who they were, and where they were going. 'Not of the race of Adam,' said the rider, turning for a moment in the saddle. 'The People of Peace shall never more be seen in Scotland.' This legend also has its echoes in *The Lord of the Rings* when the elves are leaving Middle-Earth by ships from the Grey Haven, 'out into the High Sea and passed on into the West'.

Although part of the Western Magical Tradition, we are much more likely to encounter those denizens of Otherworld known as the **Qliphoth**. – different spellings being used in the alternative traditions of Hermetic Qabalah and Jewish Kabbalah respectively – literally

'Peels', 'Shells' or 'Husks' and the representation of negative or impure spiritual forces in Jewish mysticism.

'There is a point in every magical operation when the negative aspect of the force comes up to be dealt with, and unless dealt with will lure the experimenter into the pit which he had digged [*sic*]. It is a sound magical maxim not to invoke any force unless you are equipped to deal with its averse aspect,' wrote Dion Fortune in *The Mystical Qabalah*.

The identity of these negative aspects is the 'Qliphoth' – the name given to a twilight world of soul-less entities which are not truly living, but animated astral shells prolonging their existence by absorbing the vitality of the living in the true vampiric sense. This is the realm of distortion, imbalance and atrophy in corresponding forces *at every level of the Universe* which are out of line with general evolution. Often described as the flotsam and jetsam of the astral world, Qliphotic phenomena usually manifest when there has been some sort of disturbance within the natural interplay of magical-astral working.

In more modern parlance, Qliphoth can be viewed as a kind of astral parasite that latches on to any astral voyager just as easily as a tick or flea can latch onto a dog out on a country walk. Bob Clay-Egerton likened them to 'extra-terrestrial intelligences – neither good nor evil – but influenced by the energy they encounter once brought through to the earthly realm where they can grow and develop into a more tangible form.

Looking at a worst-case scenario: how many cases of a sudden homicidal outcome may have actually been the result of possession by an entity of low grade and/or malignant ability or intelligence? For example: If we invoke the fiery energy of Mars (Geburah) into a magical working, we must be sure we can prevent the negative Martian force of cruelty and destructiveness from manifesting.

By opening a psychic doorway through which these extra-terrestrial intelligences may enter, a seeker may have no control over what level of astral entity takes the advantage. Such entities will also induce illogical annoyance against anything which threatens to interfere with the continuance or increase of opportunities for such stimulus; and will induce illogical and emotional reactions against anything and/or anyone who criticises the need for such stimulants. In more simplistic terms, these can be identified as the Negative Virtues, or vices, since when attempting to work with the positive aspects of a *sephirah*, it is equally as important to consider the negative aspects in order to maintain the necessary equilibrium. [*The Collected Writings of A R Clay-Egerton*]

These astral entities are, of course, the entropic (or lost energy) unnatural force in the Universe that drives people towards death, self-destruction, and suffering, because this level of control is what the Qliphoth craves as food. This 'lost energy' is the residue of existing power left over from a now-extinct source that adheres to another surviving, energy generating source, i.e. a human.

Like the 'lost light' in the underground tunnels in Vietnam, reported by US military veterans, it is a pocket of existing weak energy trying to get back to the light side of the Tree of Life.

Because of the adhesive nature of these pockets of discarnate energy, only a magician of Adept level should attempt to investigate their identities. Kenneth Grant contends that 'we are only now beginning to understand that these [names] contain formulae of immense magical and scientific potency'. He points out that this is also the 'habitation of the phantom forms generated by sexual desires and morbid cravings constantly produced by dwellers on earth'.

So … having acquainted ourselves with some of the more common inhabitants of Otherworld, we can see that it is inadvisable to go a' hunting for them in order to actively seek them out, armed only with a shrimping net and a glass jam jar. As Tom Graves warns, more often than not what we do encounter will be 'active and probably malevolent types', such as true elementals, 'guardians' nature sprites 'and other oddities lying around at other levels of the mind and imagination, if not elsewhere.

If we go looking for them, then by doing so, we effectively call them into existence. We haven't got room to go into all the technicalities of encountering them here, but it is a real danger that should not be ignored … and for a more detailed discussion of this, see Dion Fortune's *Psychic Self-Defence*.

Chapter Five: The Place of No Return

Once we have ventured into the realm of Otherworld it is extremely difficult to keep away from its lure because our feet are constantly drawn towards the various paths that lead us back towards those gateways! Let's make no bones about it, our magical mind is hardwired to be inquisitive. It derives satisfaction from gaining one extra bit of esoteric knowledge (though the definition of 'esoteric' and 'knowledge' may vary, this trait remains constant).

Before unfolding to you completely the doctrine which will initiate you into the mysteries, which are most profound and the most sacred, you must understand that the elements are inhabited by very perfect creatures. The immense space between heaven and earth has inhabitants far more noble than the birds and the gnats. The vast seas have many other hosts than the whales and dolphin. It is the same in the depths of the earth which contains other things than water and minerals, and the element of fire, more noble than the other three, has not been created to abide there useless and empty.

The air is full of an unnumbered multitude of beings with human form — a little proud in appearance but in effect docile and great lovers of the sciences; subtle but obliging to the great Mages and enemies of the foolish and the ignorant: these are the *sylphs*. The seas and rivers are the habitat of the *ondines*, the earth is full practically to the center of *gnomes*, guardians of the treasures and the precious stones. These are the ingenious friends of man and easy to command. They supply to the children of the Magicians all moneys of which they have need and only ask payment for their services in the glory of being commanded. 'As for the *salamanders*, the inhabitants of the fire regions, they serve the philosophers, but they do not seek the attention of their company ... [*The Black Pullet*]

Explorers, Meriwether Lewis and William Clark spent years working at it, Edmund Hillary and Tenzing Norgay climbed Mt. Everest for it, Neil Armstrong flew into space for it, and Robert Falcon Scott died for it – a chance to encounter something never before experienced ... A long tradition of human exploration testifies to the motivating force of discovery.

Evolutionary biologists have argued that in order to flourish, all foraging species must have a drive to explore the unknown but how such a drive manifests in the brain has remained unclear. Exploration is not limited to physical frontiers and foreign lands. Galileo Galilei and Isaac Newton could likely identify with the excitement of peering for the first time into previously unknown (Other)worlds.

For the curious witch, there is this hunger for knowledge, to seek what we don't know and to have a glimpse of that Otherworld. We have learned to step out of our comfort zone to look for adventures, to brave new horizons, and to add something to our annoyingly empty lives.

The hunger for knowing and experiencing everything pushes us out of the known ... with the belief that there must be something about the unknown that will give us satisfaction. Hence the long-standing motto of Ignotus Books – *ignotum per ignotius* – 'To reach the unknown through the still more unknown'.

In my formative years, I was told by several respected magical practitioners that magic was the last great adventure; in my 'crone' years I would have to endorse those statements. It's what makes us search for magico-mystical adventures in these unchartered parts of Otherworld, travelling the off-the-beaten-track for unique esoteric experiences. We're not really bothered when we arrive at a strange place during an ungodly hour because there is this feeling of danger that feeds our addiction to it, anticipating that something might or might not go wrong.

We become addicted to risk – like those practitioners of extreme sports – because the feeling of danger or being close to the Abyss makes us feel more alive. Being drawn to the unknown or danger does not mean it's a bad thing: it can give a new meaning to life. It can make us live life to the full. For society to function, it needs risk-takers as well. We need to push boundaries and embrace the beauty of that unknown Otherworld.

And yet …

… there *is* a part of Otherworld that is open to us *without* exposing ourselves to the dangers that lurk beyond that liminal portal. As Tristan Gooley points out in *Wild Signs & Star Paths*, it is possible to achieve a level of outdoors awareness that, although once common, is now so rare that many would possibly label it a 'sixth sense'.

We have become so distanced from this way of experiencing our environment that it may seem hard to believe that it is possible, and yet for those of the Elder Faith, it *is* an integral part of traditional British Old Craft. 'A sixth sense is not mysterious: it is expert intuition, a honed ability to join the dots offered by our senses to complete a fuller picture of our environment'.

Likewise, Arctic expert Barry Lopez, tells us that Inuit hunters have a word, *quinuituq*, which means the deep patience needed when they are waiting for something to happen. Through it, they develop a relationship with the land that transcends crude analysis and goes beyond listening for animals or looking for their hoof prints:

> They 'wore' the landscape, like clothing, and engaged in a 'wordless dialogue' with it. It is important to emphasise that this is science, not mysticism. It is an ancient skill, not New Age, which we were all born to practise. Without any forecasts many people can tell when rain starts whether it will be a shower or a longer downpour.
>
> They may struggle to explain it, but we grow accustomed to the changes in the sky that signify showers or otherwise. Our ancestors were tuned not only to broad changes in the landscape, but to finer ones, like the way the wood sorrel's bright leaves fold up on the approach of rain. [*Arctic Dreams*]

If we follow Gooley's direction and sit on a patch of earth for ten minutes, watching how all manner of motion will appear. 'Leaves oscillate in the breeze, sun flecks roll over the undergrowth, birds fly by, insects introduce themselves through flight and wriggling, while ants or beetles may parade.

If we choose to look, we will also see the world of the still, the shape of the trees, the colour of earth and flowers, the shade of leaves. When we stand up and walk briskly for ten minutes, our eyes may miss all but the bigger beasts and brightest butterflies. But our brain is busy noticing the things we think we miss …'

This is our first lesson taken from *Wild Signs & Star Paths* on how to begin to *see* … because, believe it or not, most of us have forgotten how to look at the world on a day to day basis and, as surprising as it may seem, research shows that we rarely see what we are looking at unless our attention is directed to it. Our minds simply don't work the way we believe they do. We think we see ourselves and the world as they really are, but we are actually missing a lot and embellishing what we *think* we see and remember – especially if we are new to the witch-world.

We experience far less of the visual world than we think we do because, for the most part, we aren't even aware of the limits to our attention. We wrongly assume that visually distinctive or unusual objects will certainly get our attention, but in reality, they often go completely unnoticed.

We don't even know what we missed because we don't notice them. We are only aware of a small portion of our visual world at any given moment, and we tend to see what we expect to see. When something unexpected or distinctive pops up, there's no guarantee that it will get noticed. If we start by sitting on a patch of earth for ten minutes …

Once upon a time, our lives were entirely consumed by looking at … listening to … and talking about things in Nature. This deep level of knowledge and understanding about edible plants or how to move quietly in the forest and get closer to wildlife, was developed out of a need for survival, and as an integral part of our ancestral shamanic skills.

In most cases, there was a healthy respect and appreciation for the complex and mysterious ways that Nature helped us evolve our traditional British Old Craft abilities. Yet today things are quite different. Most people today have barely any in-depth awareness of the natural world at all, even many of those who lay claim to the appellation of 'witch'.

Most of us are familiar with the everyday flora and fauna we encounter on our walks but what about the insects that inhabit *our* natural environment? What, we may ask, does it mean when a green beetle lands on us? If we see a beetle of a green colour, is it the symbol of good health and prosperity because beetles are a symbol of transformation and luck, while the red colour of an insect always indicates love, energy and strong passion. The beetle as a spirit animal is also a symbol of change and regeneration. They're stable creatures that represent constant progress and full dedication; symbolizing slow but successful development. Beetles are also associated with balance and consistency.

One of the most common of these green iridescent creatures is the **dock beetle** (*Gastrophysa viridula*); green with a metallic shimmer, which, depending on the light, can be gold green, blue, purple, violet, or red. They are found in heathlands, forests, meadows, and gardens with the presence of dock (*Rumex*), the beetles' food plant.

Not to be mistaken for the rare **tansy beetle** that also has an iridescent green colour and lives on tansy plants; evidence from archaeological excavation has shown that its presence in western Europe is confirmed at least as early as the Neolithic period, so it would have been known to our ancestors.

Sitting on our patch of earth we may encounter another of Nature's jewels – **butterflies** are deep and powerful representations of life. Butterflies are not only beautiful, but also have mystery, symbolism and meaning – and are a metaphor representing spiritual rebirth, transformation, change, hope and life.

The magnificent, yet short life of the butterfly closely mirrors the process of spiritual transformation and serves to remind us that life is short. This creature is also symbolic of lightness of being and elevation from the heaviness of tensions bringing joy and bliss in bright colours. Every colour has its own significance and importance and gives even more meaning to the sighting of a butterfly.

And yet … butterflies have a dark side. For one thing, those gorgeous colours are often a warning. And that's just the beginning. All this time, butterflies have been living secret lives that most of us never notice, according the *National Geographic*. They get drunk and fight among themselves; they eat all manner of disgusting things while engaging in spasmodic rape and pillage ... which makes them far more interesting and weird than any ode to their pretty colours can convey.

Similarly, **dragonflies** are also bright insects known for their vibrant colours and flying abilities. They've often been the subject of myths and legends, and have been a part of our stories and art for as long as humans have been around. Even though they are merely an insect, dragonflies are often revered in some legends, and feared in others. Regardless, they are a well-known symbol in many cultures and, in almost every part of the world, the dragonfly symbolizes change, transformation, adaptability, and self-realization.

Dragonflies have been around a l-o-n-g time (300 million years!) which means humans have had plenty of time to incorporate them into their myths and legends and adopt them as symbols. Dragonflies are also noticeable because of their appearance. They're large and colorful, which means that they attract the human eye and interest.

They are also graceful and agile flyers, which makes them a compelling creature and a herald of change. The change that is often referred to has its source in mental and emotional maturity and understanding the deeper meaning of life. The dragonfly's scurrying flight across water represents an act of going beyond what's on the surface and looking into the deeper implications and aspects of life.

It moves with elegance and grace and is iridescent both on its wings and body; iridescence shows itself in different colours depending on the angle and how the light falls upon it. The magical property of iridescence is also associated with the discovery of one's own abilities by unmasking the real self and removing the doubts one casts on his/her own sense of identity.

It would be rare indeed if our patch of earth didn't have a colony of **ants** nearby. These industrious little creatures live in nearly every corner of the Earth. In many regions, they represent willpower, diligence, patience, tenacity, endurance, fidelity, cooperation, truthfulness, and power; key characteristics associated with ants also include unity, stamina, forbearance, duty, honour, preparation, organization, diligence, focus, and hard work. Ants in nature have amazing strength considering their very small size. In fact, they can carry over 20 times their own weight. That means a 200-pound person with an ant's strength could lift a ton!

Our most common ant, the black garden variety, doesn't sting, but the UK has red, wood and flying ants that do, especially in warm weather, or when threatened. We feel a nip, but it's all pretty harmless as ants have less toxin in their sting than wasps or bees. Nevertheless, there are numerous superstitions about ants. If one stings us, it means an argument is about to erupt; ants nesting near the home is good luck.

Ants that appear to run from us means someone is gossiping about us. Ants moving East to West meant the harvest was ready; those moving West to East portend rain. Red ants crossing our path is a sign of danger, while ants moving in a row under a door indicates lies. An ant stepped on is very bad luck and may lead to all manner of sorrow but leaving an offering of sugar near an anthill is an act of charity that attracts luck.

Some of the oldest examples of **bees** in art are rock paintings in Spain which have been dated to 15,000 BC. Homer's *Hymn to Hermes* describes three bee-maidens with the power of divination and thus speaking truth - and identifies the food of the gods as honey. Both the Thriae and the bee-maidens are credited with assisting Apollo in developing his adult powers, but the divination that Apollo learned from the Thriae differs from that of the bee-maidens. The type of divination taught by the Thriae to Apollo was that of mantic pebbles, the casting of stones, rather than the type of divination associated with the bee-maidens and Hermes: cleromancy, the casting of lots. Honey, according to a Greek myth, was discovered by a nymph called Melissa ('bee'); and honey was offered to the Greek gods from Mycenean times; bees were also associated with the Delphic oracle and the prophetess was sometimes called a bee.

Bumble bees don't have barbed stings and can sting many times if they want to, but they aren't aggressive and are unlikely to sting unless provoked. Bee stings are painful, but unless we have an allergy, they're unlikely to cause serious harm. Stay still and calm while a bee buzzes around because they normally only sting in self-defence, so avoid provoking them – and enjoy their company.

Spiders, of course, are not insects but arachnids and are a remarkable symbol of feminine energy and creativity in the spirit animal kingdom. Spiders are characterized by the skilful weaving of intricate webs and patience in awaiting their prey. By our affinity with the spider, we may have qualities of high receptivity and creativity; accepting the spider as a power animal or totem helps us tune into life's ebbs and flows and ingeniously weave every step of our destiny. The spider as a spirit animal offers many interpretations.

Its symbolism has both a dark and a light side, reflecting its connection with life's many facets. All spiders are predatory and nearly all are venomous. Most weave a deadly trap in the form of a web and we may be surprised to learn that a number of spiders in the UK are capable of giving a nasty nip – usually after rough handling or if they become trapped in our clothes – but they only tend to bite when *they* feel threatened.

Numerous cultures attribute the spider's ability to spin webs with the origin of spinning, textile weaving, basket weaving, knot-work and net making. Spiders are associated with creation myths because they seem to weave their own artistic worlds. Philosophers often use the spider's web as a metaphor or analogy, and today terms such as the *Internet* or *World Wide Web* evoke the inter-connectivity of a spider web. From studies conducted by Terry Erwin of the Smithsonian Institution's Department of Entomology, the number of living species of insects has been estimated to be 30 million and at any time, it is estimated that there are some 10 quintillion (10,000,000,000,000,000,000) individual insects alive!

It does not take any great leap of the imagination to see that this natural Otherworld mirrors the supernatural realm with its vast population of spirits and entities. Except that the insect world is far from silent. As we doze in a lounger on a hot summer's afternoon, we are enveloped by a vibrant hum from the insect population in our garden.

The *cheep, cheep, cheep* of a cricket in the grass is the quintessential sound of summer, as is the drone of bees and flies as they lazily move from flower to flower. Elven-like dock beetles and the iridescent faerie-like shimmer of butter- and dragonflies; guardians in the form of bees, hoverflies and lacewings methodically setting about their housekeeping … while ants and spiders populate the darker, qliphothic realms in their predatory manner.

By idling away our time in Nature we may catch rare glimpses of Otherworld between the light and shadow, where the breeze disturbs the overhead canopy of the trees on a sunny day. And in those sloping rays of sunlight between the trunks, there are thousands of tiny insects – hovering in a filmy, mile-long column of sparkling sunlit air, highlighted by the darkness of adjacent unlit voids. Next time you see sunrays, visualise them for what they really are and let your mind fly around and through them to give them solid form that replaces the flattish way we normally see the sky.

Even the most casual sky-watcher has seen the sort of rays that often greeted us in Nature. The word used to describe them – 'crepuscular' – refers to twilight, and crepuscular rays occur primarily during sunrise or sunset twilight. When they appear, streaks of light seem to radiate directly from the sun, shining through breaks in the clouds or past objects arrayed along an irregular horizon, such as mountain tops.

While the shadowed areas between the rays are formed by obstructions, the light itself is scattered by airborne dust, water droplets, or even air molecules, providing a visible contrast between shadowed and illuminated parts of the sky. Despite the best efforts of the poets, none of their words has caught on, perhaps because they seem to describe the light without expressing the aesthetic pleasure that accompanies watching the rays playing among the trees.

In a landscape, the ecotone is the line of tension and friction between two types of environment. We pass over an ecotone when crossing from water to land, high ground to low, woods to open country, coniferous forest to deciduous, or freshwater to salt. The whole length of a river is an ecotone, a broad line when land meets water …

Ecotones are, in short, edges, hence our key name 'the edge'. This edge key helps explain the sixth sense of the seasoned naturalist. The first time you read works by any expert naturalist of the past few centuries, you will think them extraordinarily lucky; why is it that they watch barn owls swoop past and the foxes trot by, when all I see are nettles swaying in the breeze? The answer is that they know the pattern, this key. [*Wild Signs and Star Paths*]

At the naturalist's 'edge' and the witch's 'liminal space', at all times of the year, we should *expect* to notice more happening at these edges/spaces than at the heart of woods, water or wide-open spaces. These special places can also work over varying scales: some stretch for miles, others just a few metres. 'The edge is a sign that things will happen,' observes Tristan Gooley, 'and when Nature lets us into her world, it should be treated as a rare and precious gift for it will only be a fleeting experience ... and all the more precious for it.'

As we become more Adept at locating those mysterious gateways, we may find ourselves moving closer to the realm of the naturalist and paying more attention to Nature's very own natural world! We understand more about the fauna that throughout humankind's history, have acted as messengers from Otherworld, although in more recent times, humans have forgotten *how* to read the signs and the rift between the species has widened. And, in between times, humans became the planet's most dangerous predator and the most destructive animal on earth.

Humans have killed more of their own kind and destroyed more ecosystems than any other animal. The human-animal kills for sport and entertainment, causing other species of animals to become extinct. The human-animal has a big, highly-developed brain and uses it to create instruments of destruction: bombs, poisonous chemicals, bio-toxins and weapons ... sometimes in the name of their god(s). So, is it surprising that the denizens of Otherworld made a conscious decision to retire beyond the veil due to this persistent interference with the natural world ... and why humans are not welcome in their domain.

A Gateway to Solitude

This extract, taken from an article first published in Sirius (June 1992) draws on the influence of Bob and Mériém Clay-Edgeton's caving experiences, combining the two disciplines of potholing and magical practice. Here we find another gateway:

It is possible to find solitude even within a room filled with people, though it is easier in a room devoid of others. This has been discovered by many who have embraced transcendental meditation. It *is* possible to force one's attention away from extraneous noises which impinge from outside - voices, hammering, traffic, etc.

Perhaps the quietest place is in a cave or a disused mine - not the shallow cave of the hermit or Anchorite, where one still has the sound of the wind and rain, and a measure of light. Further underground there are places where water does not drip or flow; where bats do not chatter; and where absolute darkness may be found. Here, if *meta menardi*, the cave spider and other smaller creatures are in residence, they will not be heard by you.

Initially, it may be difficult to relax completely. The imagination will produce light and/or sound. Perseverance is required. It may be of assistance at first to use a single candle - not to meditate on, but to be comforted by its light - until you are acclimatised to your surroundings.

In such surroundings, time appears to play tricks, even to the well-experienced speleologists and fodinaeologists. Accordingly, it may be as well to have an alarm clock with you, set for a particular time and covered well enough so that ticking cannot be heard - but not so well that you don't hear the alarm. Make sure that the roof of the chamber or passage is over a foot above your head, and preferably wear a helmet. A sudden and strident alarm in such surroundings can induce violent and involuntary levitation.

Once you have grown accustomed by practice to such surroundings, they become exceptionally good for

91

developing communication with extra-terrestrial entities, intelligences and deities. Unless you are well-experienced in occult matters, it is advisable before relaxing to thoroughly steep your mind with the idea of the principal entity you would like to contact, and to seek that entity's protection from the attentions of any malicious spirits. [*Coven of the Scales: The Collected Writings of A R Clay-Egerton*]

Throughout Bob's writing, references to 'extra-terrestrial entities' or 'intelligences' are a common theme. For the purpose of clarification, it should be taken to understand that he is referring to the discarnate entities that are frequently encountered on other psychic levels, i.e. entities not of this world or dimension, and of differing levels of intelligence – not the science-fiction variety.

Sources & Bibliography

Taking a leaf out of Aleister Crowley's book, it is always a good move to go from each respected author to those that have been quoted in the text or bibliography: "It established a rational consecution in my research; and as soon as I reached a certain point the curves became re-entrant, so that my knowledge acquired a comprehensiveness which could never have been so satisfactorily attained by any arbitrary curriculum. I began to understand the real relation of one subject to another …" This technique often takes us to valuable out-of-print volumes that contain material not to be found repeated *ad nauseam* on the internet and this, in turn, gives our own reading and writing a sense of newness and fresh insight.

Arctic Dreams, Barry Lopez (Sceptre)
Black Pullet, Anon (The Digital Library)
Honey From Stone, Chet Raymo (Brandon)
Inside the Neolithic Mind, David Lewis-Williams and David Pearce (Thames & Hudson)
Margaret Murray: Who Believed Her, and Why?, Jacqueline Simpson (Folklore)
Nature Spirits & Elemental Beings, Marko Pogacnik (Findhorn Press)
The Mind in the Cave, David Lewis-Williams (Thames & Hudson)
Needles of Stones, Tom Graves (Grey House)
Not all nymphs are nice… Arthur Machen and fairyland, British Fairies (Wordpress)
A Phenomenology of Landscape, Christopher Tilley (Berg)

*Psychic Self-Defence, Dion Fortune (*Aquarian)
The Secret Commonwealth of Elves, Fauns and Fairies,
Reverend Robert Kirk (IHO Books)
The Secret Country, Janet and Colin Bord (Paul Elek)
Wild Signs and Star Paths, Tristan Gooley (Sceptre)
The Witch-Cult in Western Europe, Margaret Murray
(Clarendon)

Author Biography

Mélusine Draco is an Initiate of traditional British Old Craft and the Khemetic Mysteries. Her highly individualistic teaching methods and writing draw on historical sources supported by academic texts and current archaeological findings; endorsing Crowley's view that magic(k) is an amalgam of science and art, and that magic is the outer route to the inner Mysteries.

Author of several titles currently published with John Hunt Publishing including the best-selling six-part Traditional Witchcraft series; two titles on power animals – *Aubry's Dog* and *Black Horse, White Horse*; *By Spellbook & Candle; The Dictionary of Magic & Mystery*; *Magic Crystals Sacred Stones* and *The Atum-Re Revival* published by Moon Books. Her esoteric novels in The Temple House series are available in both paperback and e-book formats – all books are available on Amazon.

Web: www.covenofthescales.com
and www.templeofkhem.com
Blog: https://wordpress.com/view/melusine-draco.blog